monserrato, 20

Desciendo la escalera de mi casa,
mirado de relieves. ¿Dónde sueño?
Dioses del mar y atletas coronados,
cabezas de guerreros, bailarinas
cimbreadas de finos tallos ágiles,
Leda ciñendo al cisne complacida,
letras insignes, lápidas y nombres...

I descend the staircase of my house,
under the watchful gaze of bas reliefs.
Am I dreaming? Sea gods and athletes crowned,
warriors' heads and dancing girls'
supple swaying hips,
Leda clinging ecstatic to the swan,
noble insignia, tombstones and names...

Discendo le scale della mia nuova casa
scrutato da bassorilievi. Son sveglio?
Dei del mare e atleti incoronati,
teste di guerrieri, danzatrici
svolazzanti coperte di veli leggeri,
Leda che amorevolmente cinge il cigno,
lettere insigni, epitaffi e nomi...

¡Oh Roma deseada, en ti me tienes,
ya estoy dentro de ti, ya en mí te encuentras!
Me agrando o adelgazo por las calles y plazas
de este barrio que habito, junto al río,
barrio que me recibe embanderado,
como una barca, de tendidas ropas,
movido en cada puerta por millares de dedos,
de los que surgen, mágicos,
áureos ángeles, santos, cornucopias,
muebles nuevos con gracia envejecidos,
multiplicadas imaginaciones...
Ya estoy dentro de ti, ya a todas horas
en ti me muevo, nueva lengua tuya,
Roma en la noche, oscura voz de fuente,
Roma en la luz, clara canción del día.
Quiero perderme en medio de tu aliento,
ser aire popular entre tus aires.
Ando buscando compañía, voy
entre gatos, columnas asombradas,
basuras, muros de potentes hombros,
puertas de colosales estaturas,
atónito, adorándote, riendo,
renegando, regando los rincones,
viéndome muerto, peatón humilde,
o jubiloso de sentirme a salvo,
renacido a la vida a cada instante.
Ando buscando compañía, pero...
¿Quién se para mirándome, de pronto,
en el Campo de' Fiori? ¿Quién insiste,

Oh Rome so longed for, you hold me now,
I am within you, you are now found in me!
I expand or contract in the streets and plazas
of this quarter where I live, hard by the river,
a quarter that greets me draped
like a ship's sails, clothes hanging from windows,
drawn from door to door by a thousand fingers,
from which arise, like magic,
golden angels, saints, cornucopias,
new furniture artfully aged,
imaginations multiplied...
I am within you, at all hours of the day
I move inside you, in your new tongue,
Rome at night, dark voice of fountains,
Rome in light, clear song of day.
Let me lose myself in your breath,
one more breeze among your breezes.
I seek company, wandering
among cats, astonished columns,
trash, broad-shouldered walls,
doors of colossal stature,
speechless, adoring, laughing,
in disbelief, watering street corners,
seeing myself dead, a humble pedestrian,
or overjoyed to find myself alive,
reborn to life at every moment.
I wander in search of company, but...
Who is that staring at me, suddenly,
in the Campo de' Fiori? Whose insistent

Oh agognata Roma, in te mi tieni,
io sto dentro di te, e tu in me!
Mi allargo e restringo fra le vie e le piazze
del quartiere in cui vivo, accanto al fiume,
che mi accoglie in Gran Pavese,
come una barca di biancherie stese,
da infinite dita, calamitato in ogni porta
dalle quali magicamente prendon forma
angeli d'oro, santi e cornucopie,
mobili nuovi graziosamente invecchiati,
immagini del pensiero centuplicate...
Io ti sto dentro, in ogni attimo
mi nuovo in te, nuova lingua la tua,
Roma di notte, oscura voce di fontana,
Roma di giorno, chiaro canto di luce.
Voglio dissolvermi nel tuo respiro,
per essere aria di popolo fra i tuoi venti.
Sempre desideroso di compagnia
mi muovo fra corrucciate colonne e gatti,
immondizie, muri di spessore possente,
porte colossali,
attonito, in adorazione per te, gioioso,
rinnegante, irrigando gli angoli dei tuoi vicoli,
ora vedendomi morto, vile pedone,
giubilante per il risentirmi in salvo,
rinato alla vita in ogni istante.
Mi aggiro cercando compagnia, quand'ecco...
Chi è colui che improvvisamente mi si para
di fronte ad osservarmi in Campo de' Fiori?

fija, tierna y burlona la mirada
entre un mar de verduras y pregones?
¿Qué me mira, señor? Nunca lo he visto.
Lo saludo con todo mi respeto.
¿Qué oculta en esa mano? −Lo imprevisto.
Es un soneto. Mi último soneto.
Ma ttutt'a ttempi nostri! E ccaristía,
e llibberta, e ddiluvi, e ppeste, e gguerra,
e la Spagna, e la Francia, e ll'Inghirterra...
−Veo, señor, que está usted muy al día.
−Es el 2200... −¡Ave María!
−...79. Mi último soneto.
Me estremece encontrarle en esta plaza.
Te conozco.−Voi sete furistiere...
−Te lo digo en secreto, yo ando a caza
de un soneto también, de otro soneto.
−Povera Roma, oh Dio! Miserere!
−Por este encuentro, ¡un frasco de buen vino!
−Indove voi trova ppiú mmejjo cosa?
−En tu lengua inmortal, más peligrosa
que las tijeras del señor Pasquino.
Deja, mi Belli amigo, que en tus manos
te ponga ahora, ya perdido el miedo,
sus sonetos romanos
un hijo de los mares gaditanos,
nieto de Lope, Góngora y Quevedo.

gaze, intense, tender and ironic
amidst a sea of vegetables and merchants' cries?
Why do you look at me, sir? I do not know you.
I greet him with great respect.
What are you hiding in your hand? "The unforeseen.
It's a sonnet. My latest sonnet.
Ma ttutt'a ttempi nostri. E ccaristía,
e llibberta, e ddiluvi, e ppeste, e gguerra,
e la Spagna, e la Francia, e ll'Inghirterra…"
"I see, good sir, that you are well informed."
"It's 2200…" "Ave María!"
"…79. My latest sonnet."
It moves me to meet him in this plaza.
"I know you." "Voi siete furistiere..."
"I'll tell you a secret, I'm also hunting
for a sonnet, another sonnet."
"Povera Roma, oh Dio! Miserere!"
"In honor of this meeting, a flask of fine wine!"
"Indove voi trova ppiú mmejjo cosa?"
"In your immortal tongue, sharper
than master Pasquino's shears.
Allow, friend Belli, this son
of the seas of Cádiz, heir
to Lope, Góngora and Quevedo,
to place in your hands, having lost all fear,
his Roman sonnets."

Chi è colui che insistentemente tiene lo sguardo
fisso su di me, tenero e giocoso,
fra un mare di verdure e carrettieri?
Cosa mi guarda, signore, io non la
conosco. Lo saluto garbatamente.
Cosa nasconde in quella mano? L'imprevedibile.
È un sonetto, il mio più recente.
Ma ttutt'a ttempi nostri. E ccaristia,
E llibertà, e ddiluvi, e ppeste, e gguerra,
E la Spgna, e la Francia, e ll'Inghirterra.
− Caro signore, vedo che lei si tiene molto aggiornato.
− È il 2200… −Dio sia lodato!
−...79. Il mio più recente.
Io sono sorpreso di incontrarlo in questa piazza.
−Ti conosco. −Siete furistiere…
−Ti rivelo un segreto: anch'io vado a
caccia d'un sonetto; d'altro sonetto.
−Povera Roma, oh Dio, Miserere!
−A festeggiar tal incontro ci vuole un bel fiasco!
−Indove voi trovà ppiù mmejjo cosa?
−Nella lingua immortal dei tuoi versi,
più affilata della forbice di Pasquino.
Permettimi, caro amico Belli, che un
rampollo dei mari caditani,
nipote di Lope, Gòngora e Quevedo,
senza riserva alcuna,
affidi alle tue mani,
i suoi sonetti romani.

−Rafael Alberti

Rafael Alberti

ROME

Pedestrians Beware

ROMA

Peligro para caminantes

ROMA

Pericolo per i viandanti

A Trilingual Edition

Translated and with Essays by **Anthony L. Geist** and **Giuseppe Leporace**

Photographs and Commentary by **Adam L. Weintraub**

SWAN ISLE PRESS
CHICAGO

Rafael Alberti (1902–1999) was a Spanish poet, member of the Generación del '27, and one of the greatest literary figures in twentieth-century Spanish literature. After the Spanish Civil War, he lived in exile for forty years, returning to Spain in 1977.

Anthony L. Geist is professor of Spanish literature at the University of Washington. His translation of the Peruvian poet Luis Hernández's *The School of Solitude*, also published by Swan Isle Press, was a finalist for the PEN Award for Poetry in Translation. He is also on the executive committee of the Abraham Lincoln Brigade Archives.

Giuseppe Leporace recently retired as a senior lecturer in Italian studies at the University of Washington. His English translations include the complete works of the Italian poet Amelia Rosselli as well as a selection of poems by Mark Strand translated to Italian.

Adam L. Weintraub is an award-winning photographer, serial book maker, gastronomic and photographic tour producer via PhotoExperience, founder of the emblematic bar, *Museo del Pisco* in Peru, and the imported Peruvian spirit, *Patrimonio Pisco*.

Swan Isle Press, Chicago 60611
Edition © 2024 by Swan Isle Press
© 1968 Rafael Alberti and El Alba del Alhelí S.L.
Translation and Essay © Anthony L. Geist
Translation and Essay © Giuseppe Leporace
Photographs and Essay © Adam L. Weintraub
All rights reserved. No part of this book may be used or reproduced in any manner whatsoever without written permission.
First Edition
28 27 26 25 24   1 2 3 4 5
ISBN: 9781961056084

Originally published as *Roma | Peligro para caminantes* (Instituto Cervantes, 2021). Designed by Rubén A. Iglesias Segrera.

Swan Isle Press gratefully acknowledges El Alba del Alhelí, the literary estate of Rafael Alberti.

Library of Congress Cataloging-in-Publication Data:
Names: Alberti, Rafael, 1902-1999, author. | Geist, Anthony L., 1945- writer of introduction, translator. | Leporace, Giuseppe, translator. | Weintraub, Adam L., photographer. | Alberti, Rafael, 1902-1999. Roma, peligro para caminantes. | Alberti, Rafael, 1902-1999. Roma, peligro para caminantes. English. | Alberti, Rafael, 1902-1999. Roma, peligro para caminantes. Italian.
Title: Rome, pedestrians beware = Roma, peligro para caminantes = Roma, pericolo per i viandanti / Rafael Alberti ; introduction by Anthony L. Geist ; translated with Essays by Anthony L. Geist & Giuseppe Leporace; photographs by Adam L. Weintraub.
Other titles: Roma, peligro para caminantes
Identifiers: LCCN 2024047805 | ISBN 9781961056084 (trade paperback)
Subjects: LCSH: Alberti, Rafael, 1902-1999--Translations into English. | Alberti, Rafael, 1902-1999--Translations into Italian. | Rome (Italy)--Poetry. | BISAC: POETRY / European / Spanish & Portuguese | POETRY / European / Italian | LCGFT: Poetry.
Classification: LCC PQ6601.L2 R6213 2025 | DDC 861/.62--dc23/eng/20241106
LC record available at https://lccn.loc.gov/2024047805

This paper meets the requirements of ANSI/NISO Z39.48-1992 (Permanence of Paper).

Swan Isle Press also gratefully acknowledges that this book has been made possible, in part, with the support of grants and funding from the following:

UNIVERSITY OF WASHINGTON
ILLINOIS ARTS COUNCIL
EUROPE BAY GIVING TRUST
OTHER KIND DONORS

ACKNOWLEDGMENTS
We would like to acknowledge the people and institutions that made this project possible. Our gratitude to:
Neil and Jane Dempsey, without whose support from the beginning this project simply would not have happened;
Carmen Bustamante;
Luis García Montero;
Paolo, who opened the gigantic door of Monserrato, 20, for us;
the students in the Alberti seminar (summer 2008); and
the Instituto Cervantes, the University of Washington, and the Diputación de Cádiz for their support.

AGRADECIMIENTOS
Queremos agradecer a las personas e instituciones que han hecho posible este proyecto. Nuestro agradecimiento a:
Neil y Jane Dempsey, sin cuyo apoyo desde el inicio este proyecto sencillamente no se hubiera realizado;
Carmen Bustamante;
Luis García Montero;
Paolo, que nos abrió el portón de Monserrato, 20;
los estudiantes del seminario sobre Alberti (verano de 2008); y
el Instituto Cervantes, la Universidad de Washington y la Diputación de Cádiz por su apoyo.

RINGRAZIAMENTI
In questa occasione gradiremmo ringraziare le seguenti persone ed istituzioni che hanno contribuito a rendere questo progetto possibile. La nostra gratitudine va a:
Neil e Jane Dempsey, senza la cui generosità iniziale il progetto non avrebbe avuto prosieguo;
Carmen Bustamante;
Luis Garcia Montero;
Paolo, che ci ha aperto il gigantesco portone di Via Monserrato, 20;
gli studenti partecipanti al Seminario su Rafael Alberti (estate 2008); e
l'Istituto Cervantes, l'Università di Washington e la Diputación de Cádiz per il loro sostegno.

Índice
Contents
Indice

Monserrato, 20	3
Rafael Alberti in Rome / Rome in Rafael Alberti *Anthony L. Geist*	17
Alberti, Translators Beware *Anthony L. Geist and Giuseppe Leporace*	21
The Language of Light *Adam L. Weintraub*	25
X Sonnets	30
I. What I Left for You	32
II. Rome, Pedestrians Beware	34
III. Forbidden to Pass Water	36
IV. Campo de' Fiori	38
V. Poetic Life	40
VI. Arte Sacra Romana	42
VII. Si Proibisce di Buttare Immondezze	44
VIII. At Last	46
IX. Pasquinata	48
X. What to Do?	50

Random Verses, Scenes, and Songs	52	1. Still Concerning Piss	78
1. Cervantes Entered Rome	54	2. I Go Out to Measure Streams of Piss	78
2. Over the Rooftops	54	3. Large Dogs, at Times	78
3. Rome Cracks	56	4. Is It Only Dogs…?	78
4. Oh Rome of Gigantic Doors…!	56	5. One Stream of Piss Says	78
		6. Another Says, By Day	78
Il Mascherone	59	7. There Are Streams of Piss That Run Down	78
		8. Today Neptune Urinated	80
The Andalusian Whore	60	9. Rome Specializes in Cats and Piss	80
		10. It's Credible That Some Nights	80
1. A Nymph in the Courtyard of My House	64	11. Today a Dog Pissed on My Shoes	80
2. At Night	64	12. How the Flowing Water…	80
3. From Every Window and Balcony	64	13. Oh Urinal City of the Universe	80
4. New Trash in Our Neighborhood	66		
5. When Will All the Vespas…?	66	Basilica of Saint Peter	83
Nocturne	68	Nocturne	84
Love	70	Is It a Crime…?	86
Invitation for the Month of August	72	1. Autumn in Rome	89
		2. Rome Shrugs Her Shoulders	89
Silent Dialogue with a Neighbor	75		

3. Autumn Comes	89
4. Autumnal Venus	89
5. Chestnut Trees in Rome	90
6. I Think of Keats	90
7. You Are in Rome, Yes	90
Nocturne	93
Boredom	94
While I Sleep	98
1. The Chestnut Trees	101
2. Three Nuns Cross the Bridge	101
3. Through the Eyes of the Tiber	101
4. The Angels on the Bridge	101
5. In the Waters of the Tiber	101
6. Evening Falls in Rome	102
7. A Priest Rides a Bicycle	102
Lizard	104
Prediction	106

1. Roman Felinomachia	109	1. More Pathetic Photographic	126	Appendix	157
2. Cats Perched on Astonished Columns	109	2. Three Grotesque Masks	126		
3. The Ancient She-Wolf	109	3. The Shape of Their Breasts and Thighs	126	Rafael Alberti en Roma / Roma en Rafael Alberti	159
4. Romulus and Remus Sneak Out at Night	109	4. It Smells of Acacia Flowers	126		
5. Nocturnal Cats in Ancient Rome	109	5. Shriveled Old Ladies	128	Rafael Alberti a Roma / Roma a Rafael Alberti	163
6. Today a Dead Black Cat	110	6. Wreaths Hang from Street Corners	128	*Anthony L. Geist*	
7. Not a Princess	110	7. The Flowers and Ribbons	128		
				Alberti, peligro para traductores	167
When Rome Is…	113	You Did Not Come to Rome to Dream	130	Alberti, pericolo per i traduttori	171
				Anthony L. Geist and Giuseppe Leporace	
Nocturne	114	When I Leave Rome	132		
				El lenguaje de la luz	177
Peril	117	X Sonnets	135	Il linguaggio della luce	179
		I. Now All You Hear…	137	*Adam L. Weintraub*	
1. Water of Countless Fountains	118	II. Cats, Ten Thousand Cats…	139		
2. The Water in the Fountains Babbles On	118	III. I Step, Oh Lord, into Your Sacred Halls…	141	Authors	183
3. Waters of Rome for My Exile	118	IV. Arthritis (I)	143		
4. Waters of Rome for My Sleepless Nights	120	V. Arthritis (II)	145	Poeta: Rafael Alberti	185
		VI. Nocturne 1	147	Poeta: Rafael Alberti	185
Wouldn't It Be Lovely…	122	VII. Intermediate Nocturne 2	149		
		VIII. Nocturne 3	151	Traductores	186
Nocturne	124	IX. Time's Answer	153	Traduttori	186
		X. You Hear in Rome…	155		

Rafael Alberti in Rome | Rome in Rafael Alberti
Anthony L. Geist

Rafael Alberti was born and died with the twentieth century. He first saw the light of day in El Puerto de Santa María (Cádiz, Spain) in 1902, and he passed away there in 1999, closing the circle. A member of the mythical Generation of '27, Alberti was a prolific poet, publishing more than thirty books of poetry in his lifetime. His poetry is born under the sign of nostalgia, nostalgia for all that he left behind, for his life was a series of successive exiles. He suffered his first exile at the age of fifteen when his father moved the family from the Bay of Cádiz to Madrid in 1917. At the end of the Spanish Civil War in 1939, Alberti escaped Spain, traveling with his wife, María Teresa León, first to Oran and from there to Paris, where they lived with Pablo Neruda and Delia del Carril. This arrangement, however, lasted only a year, for after the Nazi invasion of the French capital in 1940 they moved yet again, this time to Argentina, where they lived until 1963, when they were forced out by a right-wing Peronista government. The couple then decided to return to Europe, settling in Rome, the capital of Alberti's ancestral homeland.

It is there, between 1964 and 1967, that Alberti wrote *Rome, Pedestrians Beware* (1968), a book that expresses the impression that the city made on him. The poems capture the chaos, traffic, filth, puddles of urine, piles of excrement, clothes dangling from windows, cats, rats, and rascals that filled the crowded streets of Rome, along with the vitality and the glory of the monuments, imperial ruins, churches, fountains, and gardens of the *Città Eterna*. That trash does not cancel the imperial glory of Rome; rather, one depends precisely on the other.

Rome, Pedestrians Beware is multifaceted and very carefully organized. It opens with "Monserrato, 20," a long poem written in eleven-syllable blank verse that depicts the poetic persona's descent from his house and entrance into Rome, in what one critic understands as sexual penetration and union with the city.[*] Two suites of sonnets open and close the book, and in between Alberti presents masterful poems in free verse as well as metered and rhymed verse. Some of the major themes that structure the collection include filth, scatology, dramatic poems, nocturnes, beauty, and nostalgia.

We find representations of filth in numerous poems, but it most stands out in "When Rome Is…," where a chaotic accumulation of negative images of the city ("sewer, / dungeon, prison, / catacomb, cistern / […] / seas of uric acid, / a reek of dead bodies") lead to the final, seemingly contradictory, lines: "then, oh yes, then, / dream of the pines, dream." But experiencing the stench and filth is precisely what enables the poet to dream among the pines of the Gianicolo, the second-tallest hill of Rome.

An outstanding part of the filth that catches Alberti's eye and plays a major role in *Rome, Pedestrians Beware* is scatological. We see urine and excrement in a number of poems, almost always with an ironic and humorous tone. Where scatology is most present is in those dedicated to urination, from Sonnet III,

---

[*] Juan Carlos Rodríguez, "Un modo de lectura textual (Para un análisis de la poética de Alberti a través de un soneto de *Roma*)," *Nueva Estafeta* 53 (April 1983): 35–45.

"Forbidden to Pass Water," to the series of thirteen short poems under the collective title "Still Concerning Piss," where he declares "Oh urinal city of the Universe! You / are renowned as the capital / of all the streams of piss."

Alberti spreads throughout *Rome, Pedestrians Beware* five texts that he defines as "dramatic poems." As the name implies, these are little theatrical scenes, with dialogues between clearly defined characters and protagonists (and in some cases the poet himself). In "Silent Dialogue with a Neighbor" the poet scolds his neighbor for pissing on his shoes:

> [...] Your stream of piss
> chased me like a long tongue,
> licking at my shoes... Then,
> without a second thought, you walked right
> by me, whistling a tune...

The dialogue is silent because we only hear the words of the neighbor through the poetic speaker's replies.

There are eight nocturnes in *Rome, Pedestrians Beware*, each with the same title: "Nocturne." In general, they share a darkness that is both nocturnal as well as spiritual or psychological. In one, he refuses to name a being, or perhaps the memory of a personified traumatic event, that haunts him: "The other night I saw... / Who was it I saw?" Other nocturnes express a deep solitude: "Suddenly, Rome is alone, / alone, without a living soul.' In the nocturnes we see another side of Rome, the dark, ominous side.

If chaos and filth coexist with dreams, and the material and spiritual live side by side, then so too does beauty reside next to sorrow and suffering in other poems. "Invitation for the Month of August" represents the sensuality of the fountains of Rome: "Shameless fountains that with great class / bathe nymphs in their waters / from tits to ass!" The luminosity of these verses lies not just in the sexuality of the naked bodies but also in the rhymes. The apparent contradiction between the nocturnes' darkness with the playfulness here does not mean they are incompatible. Without darkness there is no light, and without light there can be no darkness.

Rome, Pedestrians Beware is also a work of nostalgia. A longing for the past characterizes nostalgia. The word itself has classical origins, composed of the Greek words *nóstos* (return home), with Homeric overtones, and *álgos* (sorrow). It is precisely the desire to return to the place of origin, and the sorrow that creates, that drives a number of these poems. Alberti expresses this most movingly in "What I Left for You," the book's opening sonnet, which ends with the tercet:

> I left for you all that I once held dear.
> Oh Rome, my sorrow pleads, hold out your hands
> and give me everything I left for you.

Let us take Alberti's hand and walk through the streets and alleys of Rome, in Spanish, English, and Italian, accompanied by Adam Weintraub's photos in dialogue with the poems, for "this, all this, in Rome, is a poet's life."

Alberti, Translators Beware
Anthony L. Geist and Giuseppe Leporace

I descend the staircase of my house,

under the watchful gaze of bas reliefs.

Am I dreaming? Sea gods and athletes crowned,

warriors' heads and dancing girls'

supple swaying hips...

"Monserrato, 20," the opening poem of *Rome, Pedestrians Beware*, begins with these lines of literal physical movement. Alberti wants to take the reader by the hand and walk us, step by step, through a world of mythical images. Slowly, with each step, we continue to encounter evermore fascinating new characters. When we reach the bottom of the three flights of stairs, we go through the courtyard and out the gigantic doorway of the Renaissance building to find ourselves in the street, Via Monserrato 20! A few moments before we were surrounded by mythological figures, gods, classical warriors, exemplary protagonists of human sentiments and passions that make up human nature, in a universe of shadow, muffled in absolute silence, and then, suddenly outside, in the blinding light of the sun, now without cover, without protection, we are assaulted by the noise of the street, the voices of all the "caminantes," the growling of the engines of Vespas and FIAT 500s. And we are all left to wonder, as Alberti did: Am I dreaming?

No interviews given, nor forewords written.

These words, hand-lettered in elegant calligraphy in Spanish and Italian, greeted Geist as he knocked on the door of the second floor of the palazzo on Via Garibaldi 88. With a letter of introduction and two bottles of Jumilla from D. Fulgencio Díaz Pastor to give to Rafael Alberti. It was spring of 1972.

Alberti was sitting at a table in the entry hall. He interrogated Geist for ten minutes before inviting him in to share a glass of Fundador. He explained that he had wanted to make sure that he wasn't an *agent provocateur* in the wake of the Padilla affair in Cuba. They conversed for several hours, and Geist recalls being ecstatic upon leaving, treasuring a copy of Alberti's complete poetry, autographed with an iconic drawing.

It was then that Geist began reading *Rome, Pedestrians Beware*, captivated by the elegance of the sonnets that open and close the volume in juxtaposition with the couplets and free verse poems dedicated to topics as varied as excrement and urine, filth, cats and rats, prostitutes and lowlifes, imperial ruins and hordes of tourists, often tinged with nostalgia for all he left behind in his successive exiles.

When Rome is sewer,

dungeon, prison,

catacomb, cistern,

gutter, filth,

[…]

then, oh yes, then,

dream of the pines, dream.

The poems of *Rome, Pedestrians Beware* are centered on iconic parts of the historic areas of Rome: the undeniable presence of the Tiber River, the Trastevere and its majestic church of Santa Maria, the Campo de' Fiori with all of its confluent little streets brimming with local artisans' shops, the colors and smells of freshly baked goods and vegetables mingled with the stench of urine present in every corner of the alleys. These flora and fauna are the basic elements and the essence that animate Alberti's poems.

One day some years later, over coffee at the University of Washington, we—Geist and Leporace—convened to discuss Alberti and his extraordinary book of poetry about Rome. This collaborative project was born from those conversations. The project took life from multiple conversations in which Geist shared his knowledge of the poet's life and works. Leporace's interest and curiosity grew and generated further discussions, which led the two of us to organize a program to take place over four weeks in Spain and Italy. As a consequence, we decided the ideal classroom for our work with the students would be the streets Alberti describes. We would read and analyze the poems in the exact places they describe. For all of us it was a magical, sublime experience.

We met the students in Madrid, where we spent several days exploring the city, its fabulous Prado Museum, and many other places where Alberti spent part of his life before he was forced by Franco to leave Spain for the Americas and finally landing in Rome, where he lived for nearly twenty years.

From Madrid we took a train to Cádiz, across the bay from El Puerto de Santa María, where Alberti was born and raised. During two weeks in Spain, we tracked Alberti from his place of birth to the different phases of his intellectual growth as a Spaniard and poet. This segment was a fantastic experience for the whole group, with the culmination in Rome.

Years later, when we decided to formally translate the work initiated with our students, we felt that it would be perfect to complement the trilingual text with a visual element. Geist introduced me to his friend and renowned photographer Adam Weintraub. Adam understood the spirit of the project and embraced it. He knew Rome but wanted to familiarize himself with the places Alberti had made the stage for his poems. He needed a Virgil as his guide, first through the poems and then the physical spaces, and I became his Virgil. In Rome we set up our research stage at a coffee bar in the Trastevere. We spent the mornings going over the poems in order for Adam to grasp the exact contents, the musicality and rhythm of the verses, and then moved into action, day and night. What a transformational experience it became to understand how the mind and the eye of a photographer works. It actually helped inform the translations as I acquired new tools in my effort at translating Rome, Pedestrians Beware.

Giuseppe Leporace

Little did I know that this first meeting in Rome would be the beginning of a long friendship. In April of 1981 I invited Alberti to a symposium at Dartmouth College on art and literature of the Spanish Civil War. It was there, inspired by my size and long hair, that he dubbed me the "King of the Merovingians." A year later I hosted him in Granada, where he spent a memorable week living in my apartment. A number of drawings he did for me hang on the walls of my office and house today. He gave a recital in the patio of the Palacio de Puentezuelas to a huge crowd and read his poem dedicated to Federico García Lorca, "Ballad of the One Who Never Went to Granada." Our hosts took us to the ravine in Víznar where Lorca was murdered by a fascist firing squad.

Throughout the '80s and '90s whenever I was in Madrid or El Puerto we would meet. I last saw him a year or two before his death.

Anthony L. Geist

The Language of Light
Adam L. Weintraub

Smart cars. Mobile phones. Sneakers. Watches. Trolley buses. Brands. Logos.

As if these were cozy neighbors at the Campo de' Fiori market, vying for your eye and attention—"Try the strawberry limoncello with apple-mint syrup, free, no obligation!"—we're conditioned to the contemporary distractions of the everyday; that is, we hear it but don't truly notice it. In truth, that would be true within any given era. In today's image-saturated and brand-centric era, we don't consider the obstacles in competition for our attention on an hourly basis. Especially when in Rome.

With my colleague and friend, Giuseppe Leporace (the co-conceiver of this Alberti book), we sat at our outdoor table at Café Belli in Belli Piazza in Trastevere, reading and rereading Alberti's poems and attempting to capture not just an intent, but an inspiration for what might photographically represent a particular poem. As the photographer charged with the interpretation of the wonderfully expressive and visually particular poems of Alberti from Rome in the 1970s, as well as the creation of a link across five decades of change in the "Eternal City," the essence and foundations of words became crucial. In attempting to bridge time, contemporary culture not only distracted at every corner, nook, or Bellini masterpiece; it more often infringed.

In my visits to the Eternal City, it became obvious that this moniker is instead a misnomer. From Alberti's time until now, it feels an eternity has passed, and that his words are a placeholder for a simpler time. However, many details have remained—and that is where I attempted to find common ground: from close-ups to moments, in relics and relationships.

One of my first confrontations was how to make images that displace time. That is, with all the Smart cars crammed into every street, how do I show the Vespas in the Trastevere??? With the tourist kitsch for sale in the Campo, how can I show "knick-knacks"? They're gone!

It occurred to me after a few days that there was only one way to make this work: to accept where we are and who we've become—to honor Alberti's concepts, not his precise words. As many translators between languages will tell you, being trapped in a literal word-for-word exchange often doesn't convey the intent. I needed to acknowledge that just as cultural references are often lost in a word-for-word exchange such as understanding a joke, so too will the concepts of Alberti be lost in this translation (using the medium of light) if we don't adapt to (accept?) the contemporary implications of our culture.

And thus, here in this trilingual edition of Alberti's portrait of an adopted city, I try to be faithful to his intent using whatever tools (light!) the moment offered. Please forgive the wires overhead! Enjoy the occasional glow of a mobile phone! Ignore the Smart car! And revel in the reality of Rome, today, eternally changing for subsequent eras. Of course, there are, in fact, still Vespas in Trastevere.

Thus we have a dialogue—more than a de facto translation of literal words—from another era manifested in today's languages. Alberti's words continue to reverberate with stoic poignancy, and his insights are certainly eternal, if we desire to observe. Rome, however, evolves.

Rafael Alberti

ROME

Pedestrians Beware

ROMA

Peligro para caminantes

ROMA

Pericolo per i viandanti

X

SONETOS
*A Giuseppe Gioachino Belli,
homenaje de un poeta español en Roma*

SONNETS
*To Giuseppe Gioachino Belli,
homage by a Spanish poet in Rome*

SONETTI
*A Giuseppe Gioachino Belli,
omaggio di un poeta spagnolo a Roma*

I

Ah! cchi nun vede sta parte de monno
Nun za nnemmanco pe cche ccosa è nnato.
G. G. BELLI

lo que dejé por ti

Dejé por ti mis bosques, mi perdida
arboleda, mis perros desvelados,
mis capitales años desterrados
hasta casi el invierno de la vida.

Dejé un temblor, dejé una sacudida
un resplandor de fuegos no apagados,
dejé mi sombra en los desesperados
ojos sangrantes de la despedida.

Dejé palomas tristes junto a un río,
caballos sobre el sol de las arenas,
dejé de oler la mar, dejé de verte.

Dejé por ti todo lo que era mío.
Dame tú, Roma, a cambio de mis penas,
tanto como dejé para tenerte.

what i left for you

I left for you my sylvan glades, my grove
long lost, my sleepless dogs astray in strife,
in exile spent the best years of my life,
as winter settles on all for which I strove.

I left a trembling, a shaking of the soul,
a glow of fires that burned into the night,
I left my shapeless shadow as I took flight
in the bleeding eyes of farewell's tragic toll.

I left sad doves by the river keening clear,
horses wheeling on the sun's golden sands,
I left the smell of the sea, no longer saw you.

I left for you all that I once held dear.
Oh Rome, my sorrow pleads, hold out your hands
and give me everything I left for you.

quel che lasciai per te

Lasciai per te i miei boschi, la tradita
selva, e i cani sempre vigilanti,
e gli anni dell'esilio ormai pesanti,
quasi fino all'inverno della vita.

Lasciai sussulti, lasciai un tremolio
folgoranti fuochi giammai sopiti
e l'ombra mia lasciai nei disperati
occhi che sanguinavano all'addio.

Lasciai stanche colombe vicino a un rio,
cavalli al sole delle arene,
lasciai brezze del mar, senza vederti.

Per te lasciai ogni aver mio.
Or dammi tu, Roma, al posto delle pene,
tanto quanto ho lasciato per averti.

II

E ll'accidenti, crescheno 'ggni ggiorno.
G. G. BELLI

Alma ciudad…
CERVANTES

roma, peligro para caminantes

Trata de no mirar sus monumentos,
caminante, si a Roma te encaminas.
Abre cien ojos, clava cien retinas,
esclavo siempre de los pavimentos.

Trata de no mirar tantos portentos,
fuentes, palacios, cúpulas, ruinas,
pues hallarás mil muertes repentinas
—si vienes a mirar—, sin miramientos.

Mira a diestra, a siniestra, al vigilante,
párate al ¡alto!, avanza al ¡adelante!,
marcha en un hilo, el ánimo suspenso.

Si vivir quieres, vuélvete paloma;
si perecer, ven, caminante, a Roma,
alma garage, alma garage inmenso.

rome, pedestrians beware

Look not at her gilded monuments,
oh wanderer, if you head to Rome.
Open wide one hundred eyes, you are not at home,
enslave instead your pupils to the scorched pavement.

Look not at her shining portents in a trance,
the fountains, palaces, and domes that shine,
or you'll find sudden death a thousand times
—if you come to look—, without a second glance.

Look right, look left, look at the crossing guard,
stop when you hear "Stop!," go when you hear "Go!,"
you hang from a thread, your soul's under barrage.

If you want to survive, become a soaring bird;
if you want to perish, oh traveler, come to Rome,
whose soul's a garage, an immense garage.

roma, pericolo per i viandanti

Viandante, se per Roma t'íncammini,
sempre pur schiavo dei suoi sampietrini,
prova i monumenti a non guardare,
bensì lascia cent'occhi e le pupille fare.

Prova a non aprir tanti lumini,
se a guardar vieni con occhi piccolini:
fonti, palazzi, cupole e rovine care,
in cui mille morti repentine puoi trovare.

Guarda a destra, a sinistra, al vigile,
fermati allo stop! Procedi quando è verde,
vai su un filo coll'animo in sospeso.

Mutati in colomba se non sei vile,
ma se perir tu vuoi, viandante, Roma ti morde,
Anima garage, anima garage esteso.

III

Stavo a ppissià jjerzera llí a lo scuro…
G. G. BELLI

se prohíbe hacer aguas

Verás entre meadas y meadas,
más meadas de todas las larguras:
unas de perros, otras son de curas
y otras quizá de monjas disfrazadas.

Las verás lentas o precipitadas,
tristes o alegres, dulces, blandas, duras,
meadas de las noches más oscuras
o las más luminosas madrugadas.

Piedras felices, que quien no las mea,
si es que no tiene retención de orina,
si es que no ha muerto es que ya está expirando,

Mean las fuentes… por la luz humea
una ardiente meada cristalina…
y alzo la pata… pues me estoy meando.

forbidden to pass water

You'll see among those puddles and streams of piss
more streams and puddles of various shapes and size:
some left by dogs and others by nuns disguised
yet others perhaps by priests in sacred bliss.

You'll see slow streams and others running strong,
some sad or happy, gentle, great or slight,
streams steaming in the dark of darkest night,
or gushing forth in the luminous light of dawn.

The few who do not piss on those lucky stones,
if they do not suffer from painful retention of urine,
if not already dead, they're now expiring.

The fountains piss… through brilliant light there combs
a burning stream of bright crystalline brine…
I lift my leg and piss… It's so inspiring.

si proibisce pisciare

Fra tanto piscio e scrosci di pisciate
che si spandon qui per terra in vari strati,
alcune di cani, altre di curati,
e spesso altre di suore intabarrate.

Se ne vedono lente o portentose,
parche, esultanti, dolci, blande, dure,
pisciate delle notti più oscure
o di albe più terse e luminose.

Pietre felici, chi su di voi non piscia,
se non ha ritenzione dell'urina,
significa ch'è morto o sta spirando.

Le fonti piscian… dalla luce striscia
un'ardente pisciata cristallina…
e alzo la zampa… e me ne vo pisciando.

IV

Sonajjì, pennolini, ggiucarelli,
E ppesì, e ccontrapesi e ggenitali…
                              G. G. BELLI

campo de' fiori

Perchas, peroles, pícaros, patatas,
aves, lechugas, plásticos, cazuelas,
camisas, pantalones, sacamuelas,
cosas baratas que no son baratas.

Frascati, perejil, ajos, corbatas,
langostinos, zapatos, hongos, telas,
liras que corren y con ellas vuelas,
atas mil veces y mil más desatas.

Campo de' fiori, campo de las flores,
repartidor de todos los colores,
gracia, requiebro, luz, algarabía…

Como el más triste rey de los mercados,
sobre tus vivos fuegos, ya apagados,
arde Giordano Bruno todavía.

campo de' fiori

Potatoes, pots, and rascals, coat hangers,
some saucepans, lettuce, plastic, birds that sing,
abandoned shirts, and dentists, ragged trousers,
vendors expecting too much for their cheap things.

Frascati, parsley, garlic, an old necktie,
mushrooms, prawns, cloth, shoes worn by none,
liras that run and after them you fly,
you're tied a thousand times and come undone.

Campo de' Fiori, the Field of Flowers,
merchants bestowing all hues and colors,
bright lights, chaos, clamor, true love and grace…

And like the saddest king who rules the marketplace,
extinguished now your once living fires,
Giordano Bruno still writhes in funeral pyres.

campo de' fiori

Patate, pentole, gufi, imposture,
plastica, tegami e uccelli anche,
camicie, pantaloni e stirature,
affari colossali e facce stanche.

Basilico, frascati, agli, ciabatte,
lire che scorrono e dove cogli cogli,
funghi, cravatte e stoffe disfatte,
a volte leghi e altrettante sciogli.

Campo de las Flores, Campo de' Fiori,
prodigo di colori e dispensiere,
paniere sei di rumori, luce e amore…

Come il più triste re dei mercati muori,
sopra i tuoi fatui fuochi ora giustiziere,
arde Giordano Bruno di uman dolore

Ma, oh ddio, vò rrinunzià! cche nnun je torna
Da fà sta vita da matina a ssera...
                                              G. G. BELLI

vida poética

Siempre andar de bajada o de subida.
Entrar, salir y entrar... ir al mercado.
¿A cómo están los huevos? ¿y el pescado?
Se va en comer y en descomer la vida.

Ir a los templos, ya la fe perdida,
sentirse el alma allí gato encerrado.
Volver al aire... beber vino aguado...
ir al río... y de nuevo, a la comida.

Leer el diario y lamentar que todo
si no es papel higiénico es retrete,
crimen, vómito, incienso, servilleta.

Llorar porque no ha sido de otro modo
lo que ya se fue en panza y en moflete...
ésta en Roma es la vida de un poeta.

poetic life

Up and down these streets forever walking,
I come and go, and come... to market stands.
How much are the eggs? Money changing hands.
I spend my life first eating, then uneating.

I go into the temples, faith long gone.
And there my soul feels like a wild caged lion.
Out into the air... to drink diluted wine...
Down to the river... and eating once again.

I read the news and see that everything,
if it's not toilet paper, it's the toilet,
it's crime and vomit, incense, struggle and strife.

I weep because there is no way to sing
for all that winds up in my gut, not spoil it...
This, all this, in Rome, is a poet's life.

vita poetica

Vai e vieni e arrivi senza fiato.
Entri esci rientri... vai al mercato.
E l'uova a quanto stanno? A quanto il pesce?
A mangiar e cagar la vista s'esce.

Con l'anima di gatto carcerato
e di nuovo fuori... a ber vino slavato
nei templi vai perche' la fede mesce
verso il fiume si... e poi lo stomaco ricresce.

Legger il giornale e soffrir ogni mattina
se non è carta igienica è latrina
crimine vomito incenso e monetina

pianger che tutto più non si doma
ciò che nelle viscere e mascelle è soma...
Questa è la vita di un poeta a Roma.

VI

Che rriliggione! è rriliggione questa?
G. G. BELLI

arte sacra romana

(Pregunta y ruego de J. B.)

¿Por qué, señor, tan hecho la puñeta,
tú, maravilla de las maravillas,
banderillero hoy sin banderillas,
el corazón sobre la camiseta?

¿Quién en esa postura te sujeta,
sacré-cœur de merengue y de natillas,
que ya no puedo hincarme de rodillas
a ofrecerte la espada y la muleta?

Haz, dios, que Miguel Ángel se despierte
de súbito y, volviendo de la muerte,
feroz martillo en mano una mañana,

a golpes sin piedad te haga pedazos,
para alzarte de nuevo a martillazos,
cristo viril, entre la grey romana.

arte sacra romana

(Question and plea of J. B.)

Oh why, my Lord, are you such a fucking mess,
you, wonder of wonders, our brightest guiding light,
a valiant torero without a bull to fight,
your heart on your sleeve as you raise your hand to bless?

And who has hewn you thus with no escape,
a Sacred Heart as bland as clotted cream,
while I no more can drop on bended knee
to offer you with honor sword and cape?

Dear God, bring Michelangelo back to stay,
to rise like lightning from his dark graveyard,
ferocious hammer and chisel in hand one day,

and blow by merciless blow knock you to shards,
to raise you up anew in chiseled stone,
a virile Christ, among the flocks of Rome.

arte sacra romana

(Domanda e supplica di J. B.)

Perchè Signore ti han fottuto tanto,
tu meraviglia e d'ogni cosa incanto,
banderigliero senza banderiglia
che d'ogni oscurità il cuore spoglia?

Chi in quella postura ti forza infranto,
Sacro-Cuore di panna sei portento,
che più non mi è dato inchinarmi a una soglia
per offrirti la mia spada e la famiglia?

Dio, fa che Michelangelo di colpo si resumi
si svegli, e resuscitando dalla morte,
con pesante Martello in una scheggia

senza Misericordia alcuna ti frantumi,
per rifarti di nuovo ogni tua sorte,
Cristo-uomo sull'umana reggia.

VII

Lui quarche ccosa l'averà abbuscata,
E ppijjeremo er pane, e mmaggnerete.
G. G. BELLI

si proibisce di buttare immondezze

Cáscaras, trapos, tronchos, cascarones,
latas, alambres, vidrios, bacinetas,
restos de autos y motocicletas,
botes, botas, papeles y cartones.

Ratas que se meriendan los ratones,
gatos de todas clases de etiquetas,
mugre en los patios, en los muros grietas
y la ropa colgada en los balcones.

Fuentes que cantan, gritos que pregonan,
arcos, columnas, puertas que blasonan
nombres ilustres, seculares brillos.

Y entre tanta grandeza y tanto andrajo,
una mano que pinta noche abajo
por las paredes hoces y martillos.

si proibisce di buttare immondezze

Rags torn and tattered, eggshells, vegetable peels,
wires snarled and shards of glass, rusty bedpans,
worn boots and cardboard, paper scraps, tin cans,
cars broken down and ruptured Vespa wheels.

Huge rats that snack on tiny mice as meals,
and cats of every breed both near and far,
courtyards awash in filth, walls deeply scarred,
as clothing patched and worn from windows wheels.

The fountains sing while vendors shout their claims,
tall arches, columns, illustrious family names
emblazon doorways where ancient glory falls.

Between such tatter, rags, and such great light,
a hand that paints down through the dark of night
bold hammers and sickles alive on Roman walls.

si proibisce di buttare immondezze

Ciarpame, gusci, torsoli, bidoni,
vetri, bucce, catini e ramponi,
ciabatte, fiaschi, scatole, cartoni,
avanzi d'auto e moto a carponi.

Sorche che divoran topi in due bocconi
e mici dai lignacci più comuni,
muri screpolati e puzzolenti androni,
mutante sciorinate dai balconi.

Canore fonti, venditori senza ombrello,
colonne, archi, porte blasonate di colori,
di casate illustri assai glorificate.

E fra tante grandezze e tanto orpello,
traccia una mano a notte sopra i muri
della Falce e del Martello ore destinate.

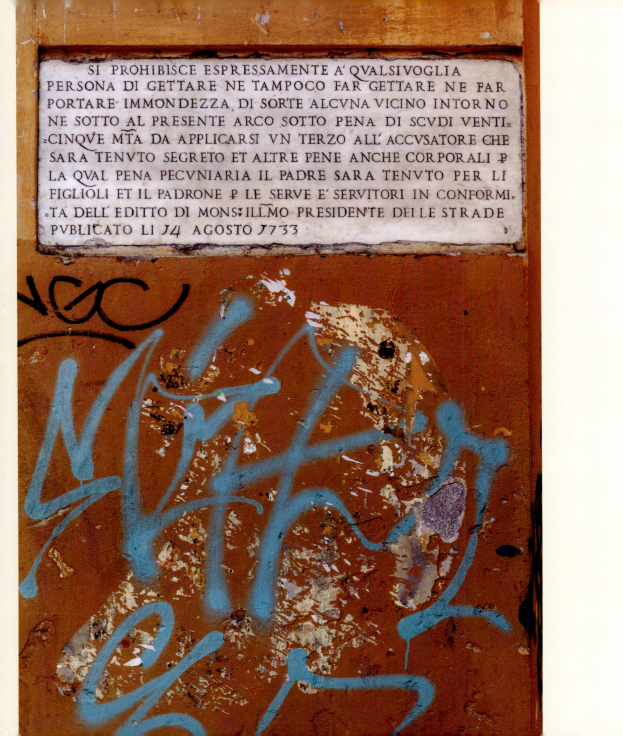

SI PROHIBISCE ESPRESSAMENTE A' QVALSIVOGLIA
PERSONA DI GETTARE NE TAMPOCO FAR GETTARE NE FAR
PORTARE IMMONDEZZA DI SORTE ALCVNA VICINO INTORNO
NE SOTTO AL PRESENTE ARCO SOTTO PENA DI SCVDI VENTI=
=CINQVE M̄TA DA APPLICARSI VN TERZO ALL' ACCVSATORE CHE
SARA TENVTO SEGRETO ET ALTRE PENE ANCHE CORPORALI P
LA QVAL PENA PECVNIARIA IL PADRE SARA TENVTO PER LI
FIGLIOLI ET IL PADRONE P LE SERVE E' SERVITORI IN CONFORMI=
=TA DELL' EDITTO DI MONS: ILL̄MO PRESIDENTE DELLE STRADE
PVBLICATO LI 14 AGOSTO 1733

VIII

E nun zai aqui a Roma nun c'è ccosa
Che ssii cosa piú ffascile de questa.
G. G. BELLI

al fin

Eres de Roma experto y bien experto
y más porque llegó la primavera.
Vas por las calles con la lengua afuera
y un botellón de vino al descubierto.

Vas via Giulia sin cruzarla tuerto,
vas Monserrato sin salir de acera,
vas peatón perdido a la carrera,
vas Lambrusco y Verdicchio y no vas muerto.

vas Foro y vas Columna de Trajano,
vas Culiseo, aunque no esté muy sano,
vas cúpula, aunque es cópula infinita.

Todo te ensarta, todo te empitona,
juras por Baco, el Papa, la Madona…
y en Roma al fin haces la dolce vita.

at last

On Rome you're an expert, an authority,
and even more so now that spring has come.
Your tongue hangs out as down the streets you roam,
a jug of wine in hand for all to see.

You go down Via Giulia, your eyes are crossed,
you go down Monserrato in the sun,
you go as a pedestrian on the run,
you go Lambrusco and Chianti, not yet lost.

You go to Trajan's Column and the Forum,
you go Colisemen, though you abhor them,
you go cupola, though they copulate en masse.

It all ensnares you, you lose all hope,
you swear to Bacchus, Christ, Madonna and the Pope. . .
in Rome you've found la dolce vita at last.

infine

Ora sei di Roma esperto, vero esperto,
E per di più è anche primavera.
Per le strade vai con la lingua nera
con un fiasco di vino sempre aperto.

Vai per Via Giulia senza un vero porto,
poi lungo Monserrato, strada vera,
vai perso pedone fino alla sera,
vai Lambrusco e Verdicchio e non vai morto.

Vai Foro e vai Colonna di Traiano,
vai Culoseo quantunque poco stracco,
vai cupola, perchè sei copula infinita.

Ora qualcosa ti punge, ora t'incorna
il Papa, la Madonna, insulti Bacco…
e a Roma infine fai la dolce vita.

IX

La verità la dico cruda e ccotta...
G. G. BELLI

pasquinada

Te quiero imaginar, señor Pasquino,
como siempre, lanzando puteadas,
siendo hoy el blanco de tus pasquinadas
un tal Alberti que hasta Roma vino.

"Dicen que es español, que es florentino,
que de andar las pelotas tiene hinchadas
y que expuestas serán y subastadas
desde Piazza Navona al Aventino.

Dicen que viene con las pretensiones
de coronarse emperador romano
y sentarse en la silla gestatoria.

Y que para evitar aclaraciones
anda con una loba en una mano
y en la otra mano una jaculatoria."

"Basta, señor Pasquino, porque advierto
que lo que me atribuyes es muy cierto."

pasquinata

Señor Pasquino, I want to imagine you
spewing obscenities in your vilest tone,
a certain Alberti who has come to Rome
today the sorry target of your verses true.

"They say he comes from Florence or from Spain,
and that his swollen balls need loving care
though from the Aventino to Navona Square
they'll be displayed and auctioned all the same.

"They say he struts and crows his boastful claims
to now be crowned the emperor of Rome
and sit forever astride the imperial chair.

"And not wanting now or ever to explain,
in one hand he leads a she-wolf dragged from home,
and in the other hand he holds a prayer."

"Enough, Señor Pasquino, I'm telling you
that everything you say of me is true."

pasquinata

Adoro immaginarti, signor Pasquino,
come sempre, a lanciar le tue stronzate,
quando prendi a tiro delle tue pasquinate
un tal Alberti, a Roma da pochino.

"Dicono sia spagnolo, o fiorentino,
che dall'andar le palle ha si gonfiate
che presto saran esposte e aggiudicate
da Piazza Navona fino all'Aventino.

"Sembra che arrivi con la presunzione
d'incoronarsi imperator romano
e occupar la sedia gestatoria.

"E per evitare alcuna spiegazione,
una lupa tira al guinzaglio con la mano
mentre nell'altra tiene una giaculatoria".

"Basta signor Pasquino, ti avverto
che ciò di cui mi accusi ne son certo".

X

Voi sete furistiere, e nnun zapete
Come a Rroma se cosceno le torte…
                                G. G. BELLI

¿qué hacer?

Roma te acecha, Roma te procura,
a cada instante te demanda Roma,
Roma te tiene ya, Roma te toma
preso de su dorada dentadura.

Quieres huir, y Roma te tritura,
no ser, para que Roma no te coma,
pero Roma te traga, te enmaroma
y hunde en su poderosa arquitectura.

¿Qué hacer, qué hacer, oh Roma, en tal estado,
ingerido por ti, desesperado,
nula la lengua, nulo el movimiento?

Si tanta admiración por tanto arte
le sirve a Roma para devorarte,
pasa por Roma como pasa el viento.

what to do?

Rome stalks you, Rome entreats you without pause,
at every moment Rome captures and commands you,
Rome holds you now, Rome clamps you
forever captive in her golden jaws.

You want to flee, and Rome grinds you down,
you want to not exist, not be devoured,
but Rome will swallow you whole, wherever you cower,
subjecting you to her sovereign gilded crown.

And what to do, oh Rome, in such a state,
ingested by you, hope lost, and desperate,
tongue rendered mute, all movement subdued?

If such admiration for such shimmering treasure
lets Rome devour you at her leisure,
then blow through Rome, my friend, as the wind blows through.

cosa fare?

Roma ti tiene d'occhio, di te si cura,
in ogni istante di te s'informa Roma,
Roma ti possiede, Roma ti doma
stretto nella sua dorata dentatura.

Se fuggir vuoi, Roma ti tritura,
ti fa sparire, sicchè Roma non ti mangi,
ma Roma t'ingoia, Roma t'avvince
t'assorbe nella viva architettura.

Che cosa fare, Roma, in tale stato,
ingozzato da te, me disperato,
ferma la lingua, fermo il movimento?

Se tanta ammirazion per tanta arte
per Roma tu diventi di sè parte,
va per Roma come se fossi vento.

VERSOS SUELTOS, ESCENAS Y CANCIONES
RANDOM VERSES, SCENES, AND SONGS
VERSI SCIOLTI, SCENE E CANZONI

1
Cervantes entró en Roma por la Porta del Popolo.
"¡Oh grande, oh poderosa, oh sacrosanta
alma ciudad de Roma!",
le dijo, arrodillándose,
devota, humildemente.

2
Por sobre los tejados, las torres y las cúpulas,
por sobre el cielo, Roma
levanta la cabeza.
—Soy San Pablo.
Y se oye el filo de una antigua espada
ensangrentando el aire.

1

Cervantes entered Rome through the Porta del Populo.
"Oh great, oh powerful, oh sacred
city soul of Rome!"
he said, kneeling,
devout and humble.

2

Over the rooftops, towers and domes,
over the very sky itself, Rome
lifts her head.
"I am Saint Paul."
And the blade of an ancient sword swishes,
bloodying the air.

1

Cervantes entrò in Roma per via della Porta del Popolo.
"Oh grande, potente, sacrosanta
anima città di Roma!",
disse lui, in ginocchio,
con umiltà e devozione.

2

Su, sopra i tetti, le torri e le cupole,
persino sullo stesso cielo, Roma
solleva il capo.
"Sono San Paolo."
E si avverte il filo di una spada
che bagna di sangue il vento.

3

Roma se agrieta con la lluvia, Roma
mata a sus habitantes cuando llueve.
¡Qué honor el de morir bajo un fragmento
de escultura romana,
un trozo de cornisa de Miguel Ángel, un
cascote ilustre siempre, venerado!

4

¡Oh Roma de las puertas gigantes para dioses!
Hoy vi salir por una a Polifemo.

3

Rome cracks under the rain, Rome
murders her citizens when it rains.
What an honor to die crushed by a fragment
of Roman sculpture,
the shard of a cornice by Michelangelo,
by eternally illustrious, venerable rubble!

4

Oh Rome of gigantic doors for the gods!
Today I saw Polyphemus stride through one.

3
Con la pioggia Roma si smollica, Roma
quando piove Roma uccide chi ci vive.
Quale onore spegnersi sotto un pezzo
di scultura romana,
un frammento di cornice di Michelangelo,
frantume sempre illustre, riverito!

4
Oh! Roma dalle porte gigantesche, per gli dei!
Oggi ne ho visto uscir da una Polifemo.

il mascherone

Asombrada.
Siempre mirando sola,
mi cabeza cortada.

¿Qué miro? ¿A dónde mira
mi pupila espantada?

Asombrada
de estar mirando todo
sin estar viendo nada.

¿Qué lloro, qué no llora
por mi boca espantada?

Asombrada
de llorar por mi boca
y no por mi mirada.

Escuchadme… Soy fuente.
Espanto de mí misma.
Asombro de la gente.

Amazed.
Always alone, I contemplate
my severed head.

What do I see? Where
do my terrified pupils gaze?

Amazed
to look at everything
and see nothing.

What do I weep, what does not seep
through my terrified mouth?

Amazed
to weep through my mouth
and not through my eyes.

Hear me… I am a fountain.
Terrified of myself.
Amazement of one and all.

Stupefatta.
Sempre sola a contemplar,
il mio reciso collo penzolar.

Cosa guardo? Dove
le mie pupille impaurite provan a puntar?

Stupefatta
di star guardando al tutto
senza altro che il nulla notar.

Cosa piango, cosa dalla mia impaurita
bocca può sgorgar?

Stupefatta
di piangere dalla bocca e dagli
occhi parlar.

Ascoltami… Sono una fonte.
Impaurita di me stessa.
Stupore del mondo e della gente.

la puttana andaluza

(poema escénico)

Señora, la conozco. ¿Dónde vive?
Por Dios, que he visto esos dos ojos negros,
esas caderas anchas, esa forma
de culear andando, esas dos tetas…
¿Que la ofendí? Perdón. Tanta sonrisa,
acompañada de tan claros dientes,
prueba que no, señora… ¿Es usted muda?
¿Quiere que lo adivine?
Buenos sapos, demonios y culebras
volaron siempre de su boca… ¡Vamos!
¡Culo de Satanás, no me lo niegue!
¡La puta de mi madre, qué osadía!
¿Qué no la he visto? ¿No compraba usted,
la otra mañana, nabos y cebollas,
papas, lechugas, huevos y tomates,
perejil y alcauciles en la Piazza
della Moretta? ¿Cómo?
¿Que es un invento mío?
¿No estaba usted la otra tarde
en la *chiesa* española,

the andalusian whore

(dramatic poem)

Madam, I know you. Where do you live?
By God, I've seen those two black eyes,
those broad hips, the way
you waggle your ass as you walk, those two tits…
Have I offended you? Forgive me. Your smile,
with those flashing white teeth,
tells me otherwise, madam… Are you mute?
You want me to guess?
Plenty of toads, devils, and snakes
have flown forever from your mouth… Come on!
By Satan's ass, don't keep it from me!
Motherfucker, such audacity!
I've never seen you? Weren't you buying
turnips and onions, potatoes,
lettuce, eggs and tomatoes,
parsley and artichokes the other morning
in the Piazza della Moretta? What?
I'm making this up?
The other afternoon, weren't you
in the Spanish *chiesa*,

la puttana andalusa

(poema scenico)

Signora, so chi è. Dove abita?
Per Dio, ho già visto quei due occhioni neri,
quelle anche larghe, il modo
in cui sculetta, quelle due tette…
L'ho offesa? Mi perdoni. Il suo sorriso,
quei denti d'un bianco smagliante,
mi dice il contrario, signora… Ha perso la parola?
Devo indovinare?
Da sempre rospi, demoni e serpi
sono sbucati dalla sua bocca… Ma dai!
Per il culo di Satana, non può negarlo!
Figlio di una troia, che sfrontatezza!
Non l'ho mai vista? Non era Lei che
l'altra mattina comprava rape e cipolle,
patate, lattughe, uova e pomodori,
prezzemolo e carciofi in Piazza
della Moretta? Cosa?
Mi sto inventando tutto?
L'altro pomeriggio non era lei
nella chiesa spagnola,

Via di Monserrato, contemplando
la tumba de Calixto III y su sobrino,
aquel Papa Alejandro que lidiaba
toros y damas con el mismo arte,
o tal vez sacudía usted el polvo
a las modestas flores de papel
que humillan más la lápida que esconde
la osamenta del rey Alfonso XIII?
¿Que no le importa a usted Alfonso XIII?
Bueno, bueno, por mí puede seguirse
pudriendo en dónde vive, si es la misma
que hace ya más de cuatrocientos años
se vino a Roma a ser jardín del hombre,
el coño puto y el meneo airoso,
desde el Campo de' Fiori hasta Sant'Angelo,
curando el mal de Nápoles
a la misma columna de Trajano y haciendo
soñar al Tiber y temblar los puentes…
¿Tendré que preguntarlo a los canónigos,
al charlatán que miente en las esquinas,
al trapero, al herrero, al carpintero,
al que dora los santos y las vírgenes,
al barbero, al cestero, al ebanista,
a los gatos nocturnos
que encandilan sus ojos
en el mudo rincón de las basuras?

on the Via di Monserrato, gazing at
the tomb of Callixtus III and his nephew,
Pope Alexander, who artfully wrangled
both bulls and women,
or perhaps you were dusting off
the cheap paper flowers that
further humiliate the tombstone
that hides the bones of King Alfonso XIII?
You don't give a damn about Alfonso XIII?
OK, OK, as far as I'm concerned you
can keep rotting away where you're living, if you
are the same one who came to Rome
over four hundred years ago to be the garden of men,
your damned cunt and wiggling walk,
from the Campo de' Fiori to Sant'Angelo,
curing Trajan's Column itself
of the clap and making
the Tiber dream and its bridges tremble…
Do I have to ask the priests,
the charlatan spewing lies on the street corner,
the ragpicker, the blacksmith, the carpenter,
the one who gilds saints and virgins,
the barber, the basket weaver, the cabinetmaker,
the cats at night
whose eyes shine
in the silent pile of garbage?

in Via di Monserrato, a contemplare
la tomba di Callisto III e di suo nipote,
Papa Alessandro, che con tanta grazia
confrontava tori e dame,
oppure forse lei stava solo spolverando
i modesti fiori di carta
che ancora di più umiliano la lapide che
nasconde le ossa di Re Alfonso XIII?
Non gliene importa un fico secco di Re Alfonso XIII?
Va bene, va bene, per quanto mi riguarda tu puoi
continuare a marcire dovunque ti trovi, se sei
la stessa persona che circa quattrocento anni fa
arrivò a Roma per essere il giardino degli uomini,
con la tua maledetta figa da troia ma sempre piena di arie,
da Campo de' Fiori fino a Castel Sant'Angelo,
lenendo perfino la stessa Colonna di Traiano
dal mal venereo napoletano e facendo
tuoneggiare il Tevere e vacillare i ponti…
Devo chiedere ai prelati,
al ciarlatano che vomita falsità all'angolo della strada,
al cenciaiolo, al fabbro, al carpentiere,
a colui che indora santi e vergini,
al barbiere, al cestinaro, all'ebanista,
ai gatti notturni
che ammaliano i suoi occhi
nell'universo di immondizia all'angolo?

¿Cómo se llama? ¡Vamos! ¿Me lo dice?
Pienso que no ha podido, mi señora,
cambiarse de nombre, que es el mismo
que desde León X a Giovanni
XXIII, viene dando
amor y gracia y júbilo y desplante
a estas calles y vicoli de Roma.
¿Lo dice? ¿No lo dice?
Ya que así me lo oculta,
se lo diré yo entonces, pregonándolo
como quien vende nardos y claveles,
manzanas y limones,
doradas, caracoles, bogavantes,
frutas frescas del mar y de la tierra.
¡Se acabó el usted, señora mía!
Te llamas como siempre y para siempre
te seguirás llamando:
La Lozana Andaluza.

What is your name? Come on! Won't you tell me?
I think, my lady, that you have not
changed your name, that it is the same one
that from the time of Leo X to Pope
John XXIII has brought
love and grace and joy and insolence
to the streets and alleyways of Rome.
Will you tell me? Will you not tell me?
Since you are hiding it from me,
I will say it then, heralding it
like one hawking spikenards and carnations,
apples and lemons,
seabass, snails, lobsters,
fresh fruits of the sea and land.
Let's skip the formalities, my lady!
Your name is the same as always, and
forever you shall be called:
La Lozana Andaluza, the Andalusian Beauty.

Come si chiama? Ma dai, me lo dice?
Non posso credere, mia signora, che lei è riuscita
a cambiar nome, quello
che, da Leone X a Giovanni
XXIII, sta dando
amore e grazia e gioia e sfrontatezza
alle strade e i vicoli di Roma.
Lo dice? Non lo dirà?
Dal momento che me lo nasconde,
lo dirò io, gridandolo
come fanno i venditori di lavande e garofani,
mele e limoni,
spigole, lumache, aragoste.
frutti freschi del mare e della terra.
Ora basta con il lei, cara signora!
Il tuo nome è stato e
lo sarà per sempre:
La Lozana Andaluza, La Bella Andalusa.

1
Una ninfa en el patio de mi casa
se tapa pudorosa las ingles con las manos
para no ver los montes de basuras.

2
En la noche
desciende un watercloset de las nubes
a engrosar las basuras de la calle.

3
De todas las ventanas y balcones
nos llueve en la cabeza
el agua sospechosa de la ropa tendida.

1
A nymph in the courtyard of my house
modestly drapes her hands over her loins
hoping not to see the mountains of trash.

2
At night
a toilet gushes from the clouds,
piling garbage even higher in the street.

3
From every window and balcony
dubious water from dangling clothes
rains down on our heads.

1
Una ninfa nel cortile di casa mia
si copre pudicamente l'inguine con il palmo della mano
per evitare agli occhi montagne di spazzatura.

2
Nella notte
si scarica un cesso dalle nuvole
a ingrassare il pattume della strada.

3
Da ogni finestra e balcone
ci piove addosso
l'acqua sospetta dei panni appesi.

4

Nuevas basuras de mi barrio: Mierda,
para empezar. Y luego,
las más extrañas cosas
a las que puede dárseles
al fin únicamente un nombre: Mierda.

5

¿Cuándo serán las motos, pero todas,
basura en las esquinas del Trastevere?

4

New trash in our neighborhood: Shit,
for starters. And then,
the strangest things
that finally can only be given
one name: Shit.

5

When will all the Vespas, every last one,
be piles of garbage on the corners of the Trastevere?

4

Nuovi rifiuti del mio quartiere: Merda,
tanto per cominciare. E poi,
le più strane cose
a cui attribuire
un solo e unico nome: Merda.

5

Chissà quando anche le moto di Trastevere
abbandonate per la strada saranno spazzatura?

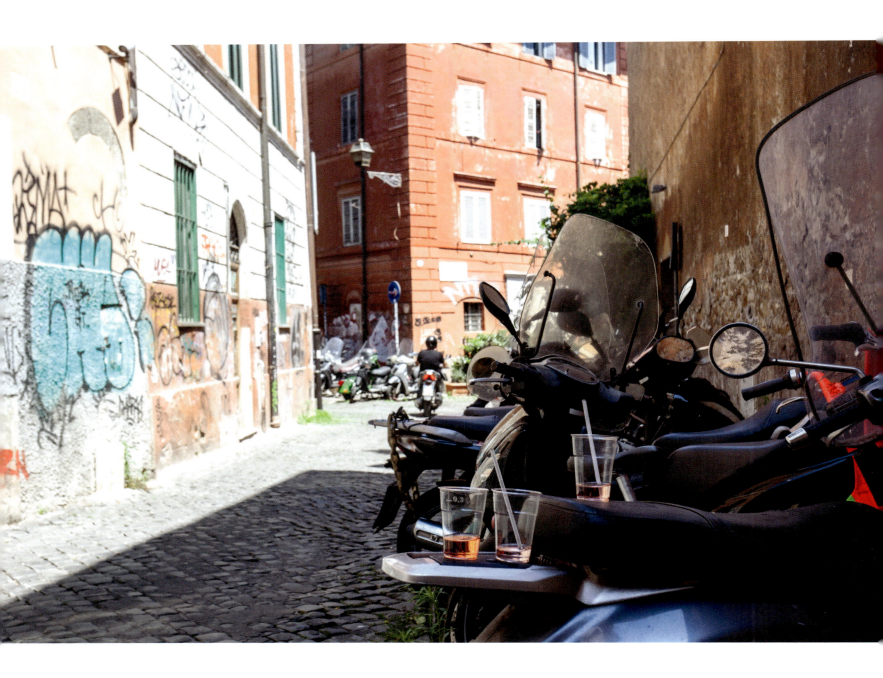

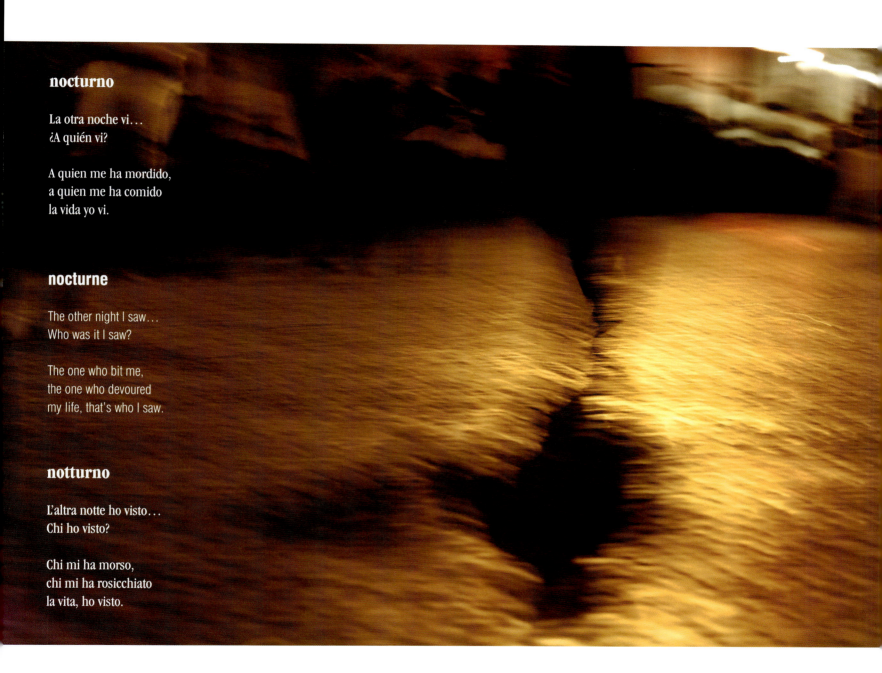

nocturno

La otra noche vi…
¿A quién vi?

A quien me ha mordido,
a quien me ha comido
la vida yo vi.

nocturne

The other night I saw…
Who was it I saw?

The one who bit me,
the one who devoured
my life, that's who I saw.

notturno

L'altra notte ho visto…
Chi ho visto?

Chi mi ha morso,
chi mi ha rosicchiato
la vita, ho visto.

En un charco oscuro,
allí estaba, oscuro,
mirándome, hinchado,
pequeño e hinchado.
Allí.

¿Qué haces aquí en Roma?
¿Es que ha muerto Roma?
Di.

No infectes el aire.
Deja libre el aire.
Si te empujo al río,
se pudrirá el río.
¡Fuera de aquí!

Gorgojo, piojo,
hinchado gorgojo,
nadie te dio muerte.

¿Quién te dará muerte a ti?

La otra noche vi…
No digo a quien vi.

In a dark puddle,
there he was, dark,
staring at me, bloated,
tiny and bloated.
There.

What are you doing here in Rome?
Has Rome died?
Speak.

Don't infect the air.
Let the air flow free.
If I throw you in the river,
the river will rot.
Get away from me!

You weevil, you're evil,
you bloated weevil,
no one has killed you yet.

Who will kill you?

The other night I saw…
I won't say who I saw.

In un buco scuro,
era là, scuro,
mi scrutava, gonfio,
piccolino e rigonfio.
Là.

Cosa fai qui a Roma?
È proprio morta Roma?
Parla.

Non impestar l'aria.
Lascia pulita l'aria.
Se ti getto al fiume,
imputridisce il fiume.
Va via da qui!

Tarlo, pidocchio,
pidocchio rigonfio,
nessun ancor ti ha dato morte.

Chi ti darà morte?

L'altra notte ho visto…
Non dico chi ho visto.

amor
love
amore

El Trastevere vive enamorado.
Los muros de las calles y las plazas
sueñan de corazones dibujados.
Marcella y Mario mueren con dos flechas.
Ignazio a Eugenia le dispara cuatro.
Antonella y Vittorio,
de tanto amor se han puesto
juntos los corazones para abajo.
Yo los miro en la noche cuando gimen
en la sombra los gatos.

The Trastevere lives for love.
Its streets and plazas dream
of hearts scrawled on their walls.
Marcella and Mario die, pierced by two darts.
Ignazio shoots four at Eugenia in a park.
Antonella and Vittorio
are so in love they've turned
their hearts head over heels.
And I look at them in the night
while cats yowl in the dark.

Il Trastevere vive innamorato.
I muri delle vie e delle piazze
sognan di cuori su di essi a chiazze.
Trafitti da due frecce muoion Marcella e Mario.
Quattro ne spara Ignazio ad Eugenia.
Da tanto amor Antonella e Vittorio
i lor cuori unito hanno
all'incontrario.
Io li ammiro nella notte all'ora in cui nell'oscurità
miagolan i gatti.

invitación para el mes de agosto

A Vittorio Bodini

invitation for the month of august

To Vittorio Bodini

invito per il mese di agosto

Per Vittorio Bodini

¡Fuentes que sin disimulo
bañan en agua a las ninfas
desde las tetas al culo!

¡Oh qué bien
el agua fresca en verano!
Ven, mi lindo amor lozano,
ven,
y clávame tus saetas,
en el agosto romano,
por las fuentes que indiscretas
bañan en agua a las ninfas
desde el culo hasta las tetas.

Ven.

Shameless fountains that with great class
bathe nymphs in their waters
from tits to ass!

Oh how wonderful,
cool water in the summer!
Come, my beautiful sweet love,
come,
and pierce me with your darts,
in this Roman August,
by the shameless fountains that indiscreet
bathe nymphs in their waters
from ass to teats.

Come.

Fontane che senza pudore alcuno
bagnan nelle loro acque le ninfe
dalle tette al culo!

Oh! Che meraviglia
l'acqua fresca in estate!
Vieni, mio dolce e bell'amor,
vieni,
e trafiggimi con le tue saette,
nell'agosto romano,
dentro le fontane che circospette
bagnan nelle loro acque le ninfe
dal culo alle tette.

Vieni.

diálogo mudo con un vecino

(Poema escénico)

Tú te estabas meando la otra noche
en la Via Montoro. Tu meada
me persiguió como una larga lengua
hasta mojarme los zapatos… Luego,
sin importarte un rábano, pasaste
silbando junto a mí… ¿Que no me enoje?
¡Vamos, muchacho! ¿Cómo?
¿Qué eso le da más lustre a mis zapatos?
¡Pues vaya lustre! ¿Dices
haberme visto en la carpintería?
¡Cierto, cierto! Es verdad.
Tú eres el mismo
que me subiste a casa la otra tarde
dos sillas y una mesa… y me sacaste,
en lugar de unas liras, tres paquetes
de cigarrillos norteamericanos…
Tener gracia, ya tienes… Y lo sabes.
Sí, pero la meada… No te rías.
¡Cómo! ¿Dices que yo también lo hago?
Tal vez tengas razón… ¿Qué te perdone?
¿En honor a qué, mozo?

silent dialogue with a neighbor

(Dramatic poem)

You were pissing the other night
in the Via Montoro. Your stream of piss
chased me like a long tongue,
licking at my shoes… Then,
without a second thought, you walked right
by me, whistling a tune… What do you mean I
shouldn't get mad?
Come on, kid! What?
It makes my shoes shine?
A hell of a shine! You
say you've seen me in the carpenter's shop?
Right, right! It's true.
You're the one who carried two chairs
and a table up to my house the other afternoon…
and you weaseled out of me not a handful of liras
but three packs of American cigarettes…
Yes, you're charming… and you know it.
But that river of piss… Don't laugh.
What? You say I do it too?
You may be right… I should forgive you?
By virtue of what, young man?

dialogo muto con un vicino

(Poema scenico)

Tu stavi pisciando l'altra notte
in Via Montoro. La tua pisciata
mi inseguì come una lunga lingua
ad inzupparmi le scarpe… Poi,
ignorando il tutto, fischiettante
mi sei passato vicino…
non dovrei incazzarmi?
Dai, ragazzo! Cosa?
Il piscio mi lustra le scarpe?
E che lustro! Dici di
avermi visto dentro la carpenteria?
Certo, certo! È la verità.
Tu sei colui che l'altra sera mi portò su in casa
un tavolo e due sedie… e mi hai persuaso
a darti invece di qualche lira tre pacchetti di
sigarette americane…
Aver grazia, e tu ne hai… e lo sai.
Ma quel fiume di piscio… Non ridertela.
Cosa? Mi accusi dello stesso atto?
Qualche volta hai ragione… ti dovrei perdonare?
In onor di cosa, giovanotto?

¿A ser el mismo aquel que galleaba,
desde el Campo de' Fiori hasta Navona,
con aquella morena de anchas ancas,
culata hermosa y fino cuello largo
de gran jaca andaluza?
Bien que te acuerdas, pícaro. Tú fuiste
quien le mostraste Roma a su llegada
y quien primero la montó, pidiéndole,
para que comprobara que no eras capón,
decirle dos palabras con el dinguilindón.
¿Estás llorando? ¿Cantas?
¿Te alegra recordar aquellos días
con la Tulia, la Imperia, la Lutreca,
la Franquilana, la Orificia y otras
que sacaban el oro de su cuerpo,
pero que viste arder, morir de espanto,
en medio del saqueo y la locura?
Grita ahora, pregona tus naranjas,
clava clavos, reparte leche, sube
una bolsa de cal al tercer piso,
pellízcale el trasero a le ragazze,
corre gambeteando en bicicleta,
méate en las esquinas de los siglos...
Tú eres Rampín, bello aprendiz de amante,
de todos los oficios, de la pícara
gracia inmortal, que ya no tiene nombre.
Alza la pata como un perro y silba,
sílbame una canción, como esas fuentes
que siempre como tú vierten sus aguas
y sólo mojan su zapato al viento.

Because you're the one who strutted,
from the Campo de' Fiori to Piazza Navona,
with that dark beauty with wide haunches,
a beautiful ass and the long slender neck
of an Andalusian mare?
Of course you remember, you rascal. It was you
who showed her around Rome when she arrived
and who first mounted her, asking her,
to prove you were not a gelding,
to let you say a word or two with your dingdong.
Are you crying? Singing?
Does it make you happy to recall those days
with Tulia, Imperia, Lutreca,
Franquilana, Orificia, and others
who mined gold with their bodies,
but who you saw burn, die of fear,
in the midst of looting and madness?
Shout now, sell your oranges,
nail nails, deliver milk, carry
a sack of cement up to the third floor,
pinch the ragazze in the ass,
careen your bike down the street,
piss on all corners of the centuries...
You are Rampín, handsome apprentice lover,
jack of all trades, with a rascal's
immortal grace, that is now nameless.
Lift your leg like a dog and whistle,
whistle me a song, like those fountains
that like you always spill their waters
and only wet the shoes of the wind.

Perchè tu sei quello che passeggiava,
da Campo de' Fiori a Piazza Navona.
Con quella bella bruna dai fianchi larghi,
un culo favoloso e collo lungo
di gran giumenta andalusa?
Ti ricordi bene, furbacchione. Fosti tu
a portarla in giro per Roma quando arrivò e
il primo a montarla, chiedendole,
a dimostrazione che non eri cappone?
A dirle due parole col tuo bastone.
Stai piangendo? Cantando?
Ti fa piacere tornar con la memoria a quei giorni
con la Tulia, la Imperia, la Lutreca,
la Franquilana, la Orificia, e altre
che cercavan l'or del proprio corpo,
ma che tu hai visto ardere, morir di spavento,
nel mezzo del saccheggio e la follia?
Urla ora, vendi le tue arance,
inchioda chiodi, consegna il latte, porta
sacchi di cemento su al terzo piano,
pizzica il culo alle ragazze,
corri sgambettante in bicicletta,
piscia in ogni angolo dei secoli...
Tu sei Rampìn, apprentista bello degli amanti,
di ogni mestiere, picara grazia immortale
che non ha nome.
Alza la zampa come un cane e fischietta,
fischiami una canzone, come questa fontana
che come te fa sempre uscir acque
e solo bagnan le scarpe al vento.

1
Todavía tocante a las meadas.

2
Salgo a medir meadas, asombrado.

3
Grandes perros, a veces,
superan en largura
las meadas del hombre.

4
¿Es solamente el perro quien se mea
contra los sacros muros de los templos?

5
Una meada dice, casi cantando: "Soy
la lenta, pensativa, poderosa,
consentida meada de la noche".

6
Y otra, durante el día:
"Soy el temor, la timidez, el signo
triste de la premura".

7
Hay meadas que bajan hacia el río,
que arrastran hojas secas como arroyos
que volvieran alegres de los campos.

1

Still concerning piss.

2

I go out to measure streams of piss, astonished.

3

Large dogs, at times,
exceed the length
of men's streams of piss.

4

Is it only dogs who piss
on the sacred walls of the temples?

5

One stream of piss says, almost singing: "I am the
slow, pensive, powerful,
pampered piss of night."

6

Another says, by day:
"I am fearful, timid, the sorry
sign of haste."

7

There are streams of piss that run down to the river,
carrying dead leaves like canyons
that roll joyously down from the fields.

1

Sempre a riguardo del pisciare.

2

Esco a misurare fiumi di piscio, strabiliato.

3

Cani enormi, a volte,
superano la lunghezza
delle pisciate degli uomini.

4

Sono solo i cani a pisciare
contro i muri sacri dei templi?

5

Una pisciata dice, quasi cantando: "Sono
la lenta, pensosa, ponderosa,
concessa pisciata della notte".

6

Un'altra durante il giorno dice:
"Sono il timore, la timidezza, il segno
triste della premura".

7

Ci sono pisciate che corrono al fiume,
che trasportano foglie secche giù per canali
i quali dai campi gioiosamente scendono a valle.

8

Hoy se orinó Neptuno en esta plaza.

9

Roma cultiva el gato y la meada.

10

Se creyera que hay noches
en que los obeliscos
hacen también sus aguas sin moverse.

11

Hoy se me orinó un perro en los zapatos.
Corrí para que un hombre no me hiciera lo mismo.

12

¡Qué incitación el agua de las fuentes
a alzar la pata en todos los rincones!

13

¡Oh ciudad mingitorio del Universo! Eres
la única capital reconocida
de todas las meadas.

8

Today Neptune urinated in this plaza.

9

Rome specializes in cats and piss.

10

It's credible that some nights
the obelisks
pass their water without moving.

11

Today a dog pissed on my shoes.
I ran away so a man would not do the same.

12

How the flowing water of fountains
incites you to lift your leg on every corner!

13

Oh urinal city of the Universe! You
are renowned as the capital
of all the streams of piss.

8

Oggi Nettuno ha pisciato in questa piazza.

9

Roma coltiva il gatto e il piscio.

10

È concepibile che ci siano notti
in cui gli obelischi
orinano senza muoversi.

11

Oggi un cane mi ha pisciato sulle scarpe.
Sono scappato subito via per evitare che un uomo
mi facesse la stessa cosa.

12

Quanto istigante è l'acqua delle fontane
ad alzar la gamba ad ogni angolo!

13

Oh città urinatoio dell'Universo! Sei
unicamente riconosciuta la capitale
di tutte le pisciate.

basílica de san pedro

A José Miguel Velloso

Di, Jescucristo, ¿por qué
me besan tanto los pies?

Soy San Pedro aquí sentado,
en bronce inmovilizado,
no puedo mirar de lado
ni pegar un puntapié,
pues tengo los pies gastados,
como ves.

Haz un milagro, Señor.
Déjame bajar al río,
volver a ser pescador,
que es lo mío.

basilica of saint peter

To José Miguel Velloso

Tell me, Lord Christ, oh why
they kiss my feet while passing by?

I am Saint Peter, petrified,
cast in a bronze restraint.
I cannot look to either side
or even stand to flee.
My feet are worn, that's my complaint,
as you can plainly see.

Grant a miracle, oh Lord.
Take me down to the river's ford
to be a fisherman once more,
as I used to be.

basilica di san pietro

Per José Miguel Velloso

Gesù, dimmi, perchè
mi bacian tanto i piedi?

Sono San Pietro monumentato,
nel bronzo incastonato,
il capo non mi è concesso muover di lato
nè tirar calci
in quanto ho piedi consumati,
come vedi.

Fammi un miracolo, Signore.
Concedimi di scendere al rio
a fare il pescatore,
com'ero io.

nocturno

nocturne

notturno

Noches que tiene dolor
Roma, ciudad sin amor.

Todo está desierto,
pasadas las 12.
Muerto.
No hay ni un gato muerto,
pues ni hasta los gatos
hacen el amor.
Se abren más las grietas
de las inseguras
moradas oscuras,
como tumbas quietas
muertas de dolor.
Sólo las basuras
exhalan su hedor.

Roma, ciudad sin amor.

Rome, city of sorrowful nights,
city where love has no light.

All is deserted,
past midnight.
Dead.
Not a dead cat in sight,
for not even cats
make love tonight.
The cracks open wider
in dangerous
dark dwellings,
like silent tombs covered in mire,
from sorrow they expire.
Only the garbage
spews its stench.

Rome, city where love has no light.

Notti in cui sente dolor
Roma, città senz'amor.

Tutto è deserto,
passata la mezzanotte.
Morto.
Neppure un gatto morto,
neanche i gatti
fanno più l'amor.
Si aprono sempre di più spiragli
dalle paurose
dimore chiuse,
come tombe occluse
consumate dal dolor.
Solo dall'immondizia
sprigiona fetor.

Roma, città senza amor.

¿Será un crimen sentarse en la mañana
a escuchar la palabra de las fuentes,
llegar a ser rumor, a ser el eco
de un susurro sin fin ensimismado?

¿Un crimen resbalar sobre los árboles
los ojos, descenderlos de las copas,
volcarlos por el césped, desasirlos
de una flor para asirlos a otras flores?

¿Andar amantes ciegos, olvidados
de la hora mortal que los circunda,
soñar que el sueño puede ser el sueño
sin sobresaltos de una vida nueva?

¿Será un crimen pensar que esto es un crimen,
cuando en verdad el verdadero crimen
es no darnos respiro nuestro tiempo
para a diario cometer tal crimen?

Is it a crime to sit at dawn
and hear the words of the fountains
become a sound, the echo
of an endless whisper turned in on itself?

Is it a crime to run my eyes over the trees,
to drop my gaze from the treetops,
let it spill onto the grass, unleash my eyes
from one flower and leash them to another?

To wander like blind lovers, oblivious
to the mortal hour that surrounds them,
to dream that the dream can be
the fearless dream of a new life?

Is it a crime to think that this is a crime,
when in truth the true crime
is that our times do not give us time
to commit this crime every day?

Sarà reato sedersi al mattino
ad ascoltar il canto delle fonti,
diventar mormorio, essere l'eco
di infinito sussurro assorto in sè?

Sarà reato distendere lo sguardo
sugli alberi, e poi dai rami farlo
scendere giù e rovesciarlo sul prato, distaccarlo
da un fiore per poi su altri fiori appoggiarlo?

Il vagar di ciechi amanti, ignari ormai
di quell'ora mortale che li avvince,
sognar che il sogno può diventar sogno
di vita nuova senza ulteriori scosse?

Sarà reato pensar che tutto ciò sia reato,
mentre in verità il reato vero
è il nostro tempo che incessantemente
ci fa commettere ogni giorno simili reati?

¿será un crimen…?
is it a crime…?
sarà reato…?

1

Otoño en Roma. Empieza a coincidir
el oro de las hojas de los árboles
con el dorado de la arquitectura.

2

Alza los hombros Roma más que nunca
cuando llega el otoño.

3

Llega el otoño. El Papa
se marcha con las hojas a Nueva York. San Pedro
vaga cantando:

—¡Al fin, solo en el Vaticano!

4

Venus de otoño, pálida y perdida
sobre los pinos altos del Gianicolo.

1

Autumn in Rome. The trees' golden leaves
begin to blend
with the gilded architecture.

2

Rome shrugs her shoulders even higher
when autumn comes.

3

Autumn comes. The Pope
flies off with the leaves to New York. Saint Peter
roams about singing:

"Alone at last in the Vatican!"

4

Autumnal Venus, pale and lost
over the high pines of the Gianicolo.

1

Roma d'autunno. La tinta delle foglie
degli alberi si scioglie con il giallo
dorato dell'architettura dei palazzi.

2

Con l'arrivo dell'autunno
Roma solleva più che mai le sue spalle.

3

Arriva l'autunno. Il Papa
con le foglie si avvia verso New York. San Pietro
se ne va cantando:

"Finalmente son solo in Vaticano!"

4

Venere d'autunno, pallida e perduta
sui giganteschi pini del Gianicolo.

5

Los castaños de Roma en el otoño
desprenden sus erizos sobre el Tíber.

6

Pienso en Keats muerto en Roma
y siempre amortajado entre violetas.

7

Tú estás en Roma, sí. Pero tú piensas,
casi todos los días,
que no lo estás. Ahora, por ejemplo,
que es el otoño aquí,
aunque allí ya llegó la primavera,
piensas que estás allí.

5

Chestnut trees in Rome in autumn
drop their bristles into the Tiber.

6

I think of Keats buried in Rome,
forever shrouded in violets.

7

You are in Rome, yes. Yet every day
you think
you're not. Like now
that it's autumn here,
and spring has arrived there,
you think you're there.

5

In autunno i castagni di Roma
disperdono i loro ricci sulle acque del Tevere.

6

Penso a Keats sepolto a Roma,
avvolto sempre in un sudario di violette.

7

Sei a Roma, vero. Ma tu pensi,
quasi ogni attimo
di non esserci. In questo istante, per esempio,
che qui è giunto l'autunno,
mentre lì è primavera,
tu credi di essere lì.

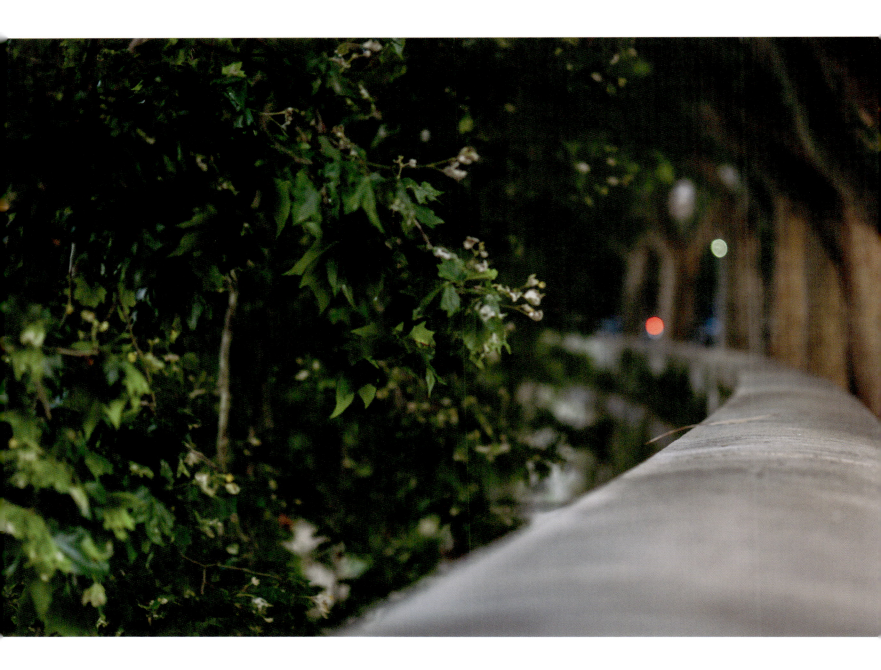

nocturno

De pronto, en Roma no hay nadie:
no hay ni perro que me muerda,
no hay ni gato que me arañe,
no hay ni puerta que se abra,
no hay ni balcón que me llame,
no hay puente que me divise,
no hay ni río que me arrastre,
no hay ni foso que me hunda,
no hay ni torre que me mate.
De pronto, Roma está sola,
Roma está sola, sin nadie.

nocturne

Suddenly, there is no one in Rome:
not a dog to bite me,
not a cat to scratch me,
not a door to call me home,
not a balcony to lure me,
not a bridge to spy me,
not a river to sweep me away,
not a pit to swallow me whole,
not a tower to strike me down.
Suddenly, Rome is alone,
alone, without a living soul.

notturno

D'improvviso, a Roma non c'è nessuno:
non c'è un cane a mordermi,
non c'è un gatto a sgraffiarmi,
non c'è un uscio che mi inviti,
nè un balcone a chiamarmi,
non c'è un ponte che mi scruti,
nè un fiume che mi porti,
non c'è un fosso in cui possa cadere,
nè una torre che mi fulmini.
D'improvviso Roma è sola,
Roma è sola, senza nessuno.

el aburrimiento
(poema escénico)

boredom
(dramatic poem)

la noia
(poema scenico)

Me aburro.

Me aburro.

Me aburro.

¡Cómo en Roma me aburro!

Más que nunca me aburro.

Estoy muy aburrido.

¡Qué aburrido que estoy!

Quiero decir de todas las maneras

lo aburrido que estoy.

Todos ven en mi cara mi gran aburrimiento.

Innegable, señor.

Es indisimulable.

¿Está usted aburrido?

Me parece que está usted muy aburrido.

Dígame, ¿a dónde va tan aburrido?

¿Que usted va a las iglesias con ese aburrimiento?

No es posible, señor, que vaya a las iglesias

con ese aburrimiento.

¿Que a los museos —dice— siendo tan aburrido?

¿Quién no siente en mi andar lo aburrido que estoy?

I'm bored.

I'm bored.

I'm bored.

Rome bores me so!

I've never been so bored in my life.

I'm very bored.

I'm so damned bored!

I want to say every possible way

how bored I am.

Everyone can see great boredom in my face.

It's undeniable, sir.

You can't hide it.

Are you bored?

You seem extremely bored.

Tell me, where are you going so bored?

You're visiting churches with that boredom?

It's not possible, sir, to visit churches

with such boredom.

To museums, you say, while you're so bored?

Is there anyone who can't see in my gait how bored I am?

M'annoio.

M'annoio.

M'annoio.

Roma m'annoia così tanto!

Mai sentita tanta noia in vita.

Sono così annoiato!

Quanto sono annoiato!

Vorrei trovare le parole adatte

a descrivere la mia noia.

Tutti possono leggermi in faccia la mia noia.

È innegabile, caro signore.

impossibile da nascondere.

Anche lei soffre la stessa noia?

Ho l'impressione che anche lei sia molto annoiato.

Mi dica, dove va in compagnia di tanta noia?

Lei va a visitare le chiese con tanta noia in viso?

Signore, non è possibile che lei vada in chiesa

con tanta noia in faccia.

Va ai musei —dice-- mentre è così annoiato?

Chi non riesce a vedere nei miei passi quanto io sia

annoiato?

¡Qué aire de aburrimiento!
A la legua se ve su gran aburrimiento.
Mi gran aburrimiento.
Lo aburrido que estoy.
Y sin embargo… ¡Oooh!
He pisado una caca…
Acabo de pisar –¡santo Dios!– una caca…
Dicen que trae suerte el pisar una caca…
Que trae mucha suerte el pisar una caca…
¿Suerte, señores, suerte?
¿La suerte… la… la suerte?
Estoy pegado al suelo.
No puedo caminar.
Ahora sí que ya nunca volveré a caminar.
Me aburro, ay, me aburro.
Más que nunca me aburro.
Muero de aburrimiento.
No hablo más…

        Me morí.

Such an air of boredom!
You can see your great boredom a mile away.
My great boredom.
How bored I am.
And yet… Oooh!
I stepped in shit…
Holy God! I just stepped in shit…
They say it's good luck to step in shit…
Great good luck to step in shit…
Good luck, ladies and gentlemen, good luck?
Luck… lu… lu… luck?
I'm stuck to the sidewalk.
I can't walk.
I'll never be able to walk again.
I'm bored, oh, I'm bored.
I've never been so bored.
I'm dying of boredom.
I'll say no more…

        I died.

Che aria di noia!
La tua noia si vede da lontano.
La mia grande noia.
Sono così annoiato.
E poi… Oooh!
Ho pestato una cacca…
Santo Dio! Ho pestato una cacca…
Si dice che porti fortuna calpestare cacca…
Grande fortuna calpestare una cacca…
Buona fortuna, signori, buona fortuna?
La fortuna… la… la fortuna?
Sono incollato all'asfalto.
Non posso più camminare.
Non potrò mai più camminare.
Sono pieno di noia, oh, tanta noia.
Mai più mi sentirò tanto divorato dalla noia.
Mi sto spegnendo dalla noia.
Non dirò più nulla…

        Son morto.

mientras duermo

Mientras duermo,
las campanas del Trastevere
van y vienen por mi sueño.

Ya vienen, ya van.
¡Señor, qué trabajo
mueve el sacristán!
En cada badajo
repica un carajo
tin ton y tin tan.

Mientras duermo,
las campanas del Trastevere
vienen y van.

while i sleep

While I sleep,
the bells of the Trastevere
in my dreams, they come and go.

Now they come, now they go.
Lord, how the sexton
strains to make them ring!
In each clapper
rings a snapper
ding dong, dong ding.

While I sleep,
the bells of the Trastevere
in my dreams, they go and come.

mentre dormo

Mentre dormo,
le campane di Trastevere
nei miei sogni vengon e van.

Vengon e van.
Dio che fatica che
deve fare il sacrestan!
Per ogni colpo
la voce di uno stolto
din don din dan.

Mentre dormo,
le campane di Trastevere
vengon e van.

1

Los castaños del Sena
han bajado esa noche a ver el Tíber.

2

Pasan tres monjas por el puente. El Tíber
ha visto tantas, que ni las refleja.

3

Por los ojos del Tíber pasan hoy
todos los muertos de su larga historia.

4

Quieren esta mañana
los ángeles del puente
volar sobre el castillo de Sant'Angelo.

5

En las aguas de Tíber esta noche
lloraba Miguel Ángel.

1

The chestnut trees that line the Seine
came down tonight to visit the Tiber.

2

Three nuns cross the bridge. The Tiber
has seen so many it doesn't bother to show their reflection.

3

Through the eyes of the Tiber all the dead
in its long history flow by today.

4

The angels on the bridge
this morning long
to fly over Castel Sant'Angelo.

5

In the waters of the Tiber
Michelangelo wept tonight.

1

I castagni della Senna
stanotte sono scesi a far visita al Tevere.

2

Tre monache passano sul ponte. Le acque del Tevere
tante ne han viste che non le riflette più.

3

Oggi sotto gli occhi del Tevere passano
tutti i morti della sua lunga storia.

4

Questa mattina
gli angeli del ponte desiderano
volare sopra Castel Sant'Angelo.

5

Questa notte nelle acque del Tevere
Michelangelo ha pianto.

6

Cae en Roma la tarde. Tres curas colorados
pasan bajo los arcos, camino del crepúsculo.

7

Un cura en bicicleta por el puente.
Yo ya no tengo bicicleta. ¿Acaso
tendré que hacerme cura
para tener de nuevo bicicleta?

6

Evening falls in Rome. Three red-robed priests
walk through the arches, trudging toward dusk.

7

A priest rides a bicycle over the bridge.
I no longer have a bicycle. Must I
become a priest
to have a bike again?

6

Su Roma cala il vespro. Tre curati colorati
attraverso gli archi, entrano nel crepuscolo.

7

Un prete in bicicletta sul ponte.
Io non possiedo più una bicicletta. Dovrò far
il prete per avere
di nuovo una bicicletta?

lagartija
lizard
la lucertola

Lagartija romana,
al sol por los tejados.
¿Bajo qué humilde teja
escondes tu palacio?

Ya eres de bronce verde,
ya de oro azul opaco.
¿De qué orfebre has salido,
en qué cuello has soñado?

Fija, miras el cielo,
los árboles lejanos,
las torres y las cúpulas,
los muros agrietados.
Luego, graciosamente,
te alejas, paseando.

Lizard of Rome,
basking on the rooftops.
What humble tile
hides your palace home?

One moment shimmering bronze,
at others opaque blue gold.
What throat do you caress in your dreams,
what goldsmith crafted you bold?

Motionless, you stare at the sky,
the distant trees,
the towers and domes,
the crumbling walls.
Then, gracefully, strolling
by, you move on.

Lucertola romana,
al sole sui tetti.
Sotto quale tegola
si nasconde il tuo palazzo?

A volte sembri bronzo-verde,
ed altre di opaco azzurro-oro.
Da quale orafo sei nata,
quale collo ti ha sognata?

Occhi fissi, rivolti al cielo,
agli alberi distanti,
le torri e le cupole,
i muri lesinanti.
Poi, graziosamente,
prosegui, passeggiando.

predicción

¿Yo en el umbral de la vejez? ¡Qué risa!
En vísperas alegres de cumplir
los 66 años aquí en Roma,
soy tan joven y fuerte como Roma,
y sólo moriré con toda Roma,
cuando el caballo, verde todavía,
de Marco Aurelio, vuelva
de nuevo a ser dorado.

prediction

I'm on the threshold of old age? That's a laugh!
On the joyful eve of turning
66 here in Rome.
I'm as young and strong as Rome,
and I'll only die with Rome itself,
when Marcus Aurelius's horse,
now tarnished green, once more
turns gold.

predizione

Sono al tramonto dei miei anni? Che scompisciatura!
alla vigilia, felice, di compiere
i miei 66 qui a Roma,
mi sento ancora giovane e forte quanto Roma,
e morirò solo quando morirà Roma,
quando il cavallo di Marco Aurelio,
ancora verde, ritornerà
nuovamente ad essere dorato.

1

Gatomaquia romana. ¡Qué poema
hubiera escrito aquí Lope de Vega!

2

Gatos en las columnas asombradas.

3

La vieja loba madre
ha sido derrotada por los gatos.

4

Rómulo y Remo bajan por la noche
para mamar la leche de las gatas
y jugar con los gatos por los Foros.

5

Gatos nocturnos en la Roma antigua.
Parecen esperar entre las sombras
la caricia sonámbula
de Baudelaire.

1

Roman felinomachia. What a poem
Lope de Vega would have written!

2

Cats perched on astonished columns.

3

The ancient she-wolf
has been vanquished by cats.

4

Romulus and Remus sneak out at night
to suckle on the milk of cats
and play with kittens in the Forum.

5

Nocturnal cats in ancient Rome.
They lurk in the shadows awaiting
Baudelaire's
sleepy caress.

1

Gattomachia romana: che poema
avrebbe scritto qui Lope de Vega!

2

Gatti sulle colonne stupefatte.

3

La vecchia lupa
scacciata dai gatti.

4

Di notte Romolo e Remo escono
a succhiar tette di gatte
e a giocare coi gatti nei Fori.

5

Gatti notturni nell'antica Roma.
Sembra aspettino nell'ombra
Le sonnambule carezze
di Baudelaire.

6

Hoy me pasó rozándome la frente
un gato muerto negro.
Venía
de la última ventana de un palacio.

7

En vez de la princesa,
en vez del duque,
hoy sale por la puerta derruida
un gran gato sarnoso.

6

Today a dead black cat
brushed across my forehead,
flung
from the highest window of a palazzo.

7

Not a princess,
not a duke,
but a huge mangy cat struts
through the crumbling doorway today.

6

Oggi un gatto nero morto
mi ha sfiorato la fronte.
Proveniva
dall'ultima finestra di un palazzo.

7

Invece della principessa,
invece del duca,
oggi viene fuori dalla porta sguaiata
un enorme gatto rognoso.

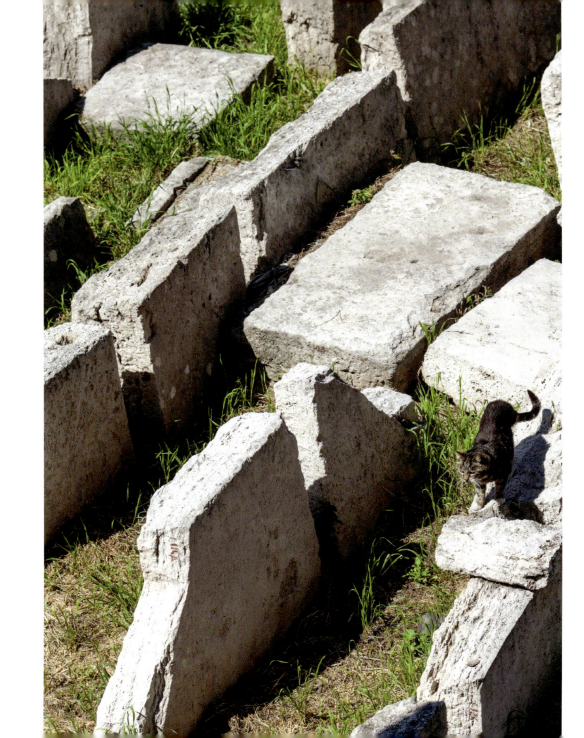

cuando roma es…

Cuando Roma es cloaca,
mazmorra, calabozo,
catacumba, cisterna,
albañal, inmundicias,
ventanas rotas, grietas,
cornisas que se caen,
gente enana, tremendas
barrigas de ocho meses,
explosiones, estruendo,
ruidos que te degüellan,
rodados que te aplastan,
monstruos que te apretujan,
sombras que te cohíben,
escombros que te estrechan,
mares de ácido úrico,
bocanadas de muertos
hedores, pesadillas
de siglos barajados,
montón de huesos, piedras,
desolados olvidos,
piedras difuntas, piedras…
entonces, oh, sí, entonces,
sueña en los pinos, sueña.

when rome is…

When Rome is sewer,
dungeon, prison,
catacomb, cistern,
gutter, filth,
shattered windows, cracks,
cornices that crumble,
tiny people, swollen
bellies eight months pregnant,
explosions, thunder,
sounds that behead you,
vehicles that smash you,
monsters that crush you,
shadows that terrify you,
rubble that squashes you,
seas of uric acid,
a reek of dead bodies,
stench, nightmares shuffled
through centuries,
mounds of bones, stones,
desolate oblivion,
defunct stones, stones…
then, oh yes, then,
dream of the pines, dream.

quando roma è…

Quando Roma è cloaca,
gattabuia, carcere,
catacomba, cisterna,
latrina, immondezzaio,
rotte finestre, crepe,
frantumi di cornicioni,
gente nana, pancioni
di otto mesi,
esplosioni, fragore,
frastuono che ti sgozzano,
veicoli che ti schiacciano,
mostri che ti strusciano,
ombre che ti minacciano,
macerie che ti affogano,
mari di acido urico,
boccate di morti,
fetori, angosce
di secoli rimescolati,
montagne di ossa, massi,
desolati oblii,
pietre defunte, pietre…
quindi, oh, sì, quindi,
sogna i tuoi pini, sogna.

nocturno

Está vacía Roma, de pronto. Está sin nadie.
Sólo piedras y grietas. Soledad y silencio.
Hoy la terrible madre de todos los ruidos
yace ante mí callada igual que un camposanto.
Como un borracho, a tumbos, ando no sé por dónde.
Me he quedado sin sombra, porque todo está a oscuras.
La busco y no la encuentro. Es la primera noche
de mi vida en que ha huido la sombra de mi lado.
No adivino las puertas, no adivino los muros.
Todo es como una inmensa catacumba cerrada.
Ha muerto el agua, han muerto las voces y los pasos.
No sé quién soy e ignoro hacia dónde camino.
La sangre se me agolpa en mitad de la lengua.
Roma me sabe a sangre y a borbotón la escupo.
Cruje, salta, se rompe, se derrumba, se cae.
Sólo un hoyo vacío me avisa en las tinieblas
lo que me está esperando.

nocturne

Suddenly, Rome is empty. No one in sight.
Only stones and crevices. Solitude and silence.
Today the terrible mother of all sounds
lies before me, silent as a graveyard.
Stumbling like a drunk, I know not where I wander.
I have lost my shadow, for all is dark.
I look for it and do not find it. It is the first night
of my life when my shadow has fled from my side.
I can't make out the doors, I can't make out the walls.
Everything is like an immense sealed catacomb.
The water has died, voices and footsteps have died.
I don't know who I am or where I'm going.
My blood pools in the middle of my tongue.
Rome tastes like blood and I spit it out in spurts.
It crumbles, leaps, fractures, tumbles, falls.
Only a hollow pit in the darkness foretells
what awaits me.

notturno

All'improvviso Roma è un deserto. Non c'è anima viva.
Solo pietre e crepe. Silenzio e solitudine.
Oggi come in un silente camposanto
ho davanti l'implacabile madre dei rumori.
Come un ubriaco, arrembando, proseguo senza meta.
Non intravedo la mia stessa ombra, perchè tutto è buio.
La cerco, ma non la vedo. È la prima notte in
vita mia che la mia ombra non mi è a fianco.
Non riconosco più le porte, non riconosco i muri.
Tutto è come un'immensa catacomba sigillata.
L'acqua è morta, morti sono passi e voci.
Non so chi io sia e dove stia andando.
Il mio sangue sgorga dal mezzo della lingua.
Roma mi sa di sangue che sputo a fiotti.
Schricchiola, salta, si sgretola, vien giù, cade.
Soltanto una vuota buca mi annuncia nel buio
ciò che mi aspetta.

peligro

De las ventanas vacías,
la voz de los siglos muertos
baja, callada, en la noche.
Pero al lado vive alguien,
algunos que están durmiendo
tranquilamente en alcobas
que han salvado de la muerte.
Mas hay siempre la amenaza
de un esqueleto astillado
que no duerme.

peril

Slithering from empty windows
the voice of centuries long dead
descends, silent, into the night.
But someone lives nearby,
someone sleeping
peacefully in a bed
salvaged from the hands of death.
But the threat
of a splintered skeleton,
sleepless, still looms.

pericolo

Finestre vuote da cui
proviene muta nella notte,
la voce di morti secoli.
Ma a fianco vi vive qualcuno,
qualcuno che dorme
serenamente nei letti
sottratti alla morte.
Ma persiste la minaccia
di uno scheggiato scheletro
che veglia.

1

El agua de las fuentes innumerables. Duermo
oyendo su infinito
resonar. Agua es
aquí en Roma mi sueño.

2

Sigue charlando el agua de las fuentes
completamente ajena
a todo, indiferente.
Lo que dice es tan sólo lo que suena.

3

Agua de Roma para mi destierro,
para mi corazón
fuera de sus dominios tantas veces.

1

Water of countless fountains. I hear
its endless splashing
in my sleep. Water is
my sleep here n Rome.

2

The water in the fountains babbles on,
totally distant
from everything, indifferent.
What it means is just what you hear.

3

Waters of Rome for my exile,
for my heart
so often distant from its domain.

1

L'acqua di innumerevoli fontane. Dormo
ascoltando il suo infinito
risuonare. L'acqua è
qui in Roma il mio sogno.

2

Incessante il chiacchierio dell'acqua delle fontane,
completamente alieno
a tutto, indifferente.
Ciò che ripete è il suo stesso suono.

3

Acqua di Roma per il mio esilio,
per il mio cuore
così spesso lontano dal suo regno.

4
Agua de Roma para mis insomnios,
esos largos oscuros en que pueblo los techos
de mí, mudas imágenes,
que apenas si conozco.
Agua para los pobres, los mendigos,
esos que se abandonan al borde de las fuentes
y se quedan dormidos.
Agua para los perros vagabundos,
para todas las bocas sedientas, de pasada,
agua para las flores y los pájaros,
para los peces silenciosos, agua
para el cielo volcado con sus nubes,
con su luna, su sol y sus estrellas.
Pero por sobre todo,
agua sólo sonido, repetición constante,
agua sueño sin fin,
agua eterna de Roma.
Agua.

4

Waters of Rome for my sleepless nights,
so long and dark when I populate the rooftops
with myself, mute images
that I scarcely recognize.
Water for the poor, beggars,
who lie down on the edge of fountains
and sleep.
Water for stray dogs,
for all the thirsty mouths, as well,
water for flowers and birds,
for silent fish, water
for the sky with its tumbling clouds,
its moon, its sun and stars.
But most all,
water that is just sound, constant repetition,
water endless dream,
eternal waters of Rome.
Water.

4

Acqua di Roma per le mie notti insonni,
così lunghe e buie quando io popolo i tetti
di me stesso, immagini mute,
che appena riconosco.
Acqua per i poveri, i mendicanti,
quelli che si abbandonano sui bordi delle fontane
e che si addormentano.
Acqua per i cani randagi,
per tutte le bocche assetate, di passaggio,
acqua per i fiori e gli uccelli,
per i pesci silenziosi, acqua
per il cielo solcato dalle sue nuvole,
con la sua luna, il suo sole e le sue stelle.
Ma sopra ogni cosa,
acqua solo suono, costante ripetizione,
acqua sogno senza fine,
acqua eterna di Roma.
Acqua.

sería tan hermoso…
wouldn't it be lovely…
come sarebbe bello…

Sería tan hermoso estar—aquí—tranquilo,
el mundo en paz con todo,
escuchando esta fuente en la mañana
sin pensar que su voz abierta y pura
cae para mí quebrada en mil lamentos,
que en sus diez inhibidos surtidores
para mí se estremece un mar de sangre.

¡Oh cerrado jardín inmóvil que me ofrece
tanta apariencia de sosiego, tanto
anhelo de una vida
calma por fin, por fin, por fin serena!

Mas no es así, pues oigo
en el más leve céfiro que roza
las flores y los árboles
un resonar de carros armados, un estruendo
de muerte descendida de los cielos, llegada
de todas partes, una
larga noche de heridos y doblados
para siempre en la tierra.

Wouldn't it be lovely to be—here—at ease,
the world at peace with everything,
to hear this fountain in the morning
and not think that its pure, open voice
will shatter for me into a thousand laments,
that in its ten gentle spouts
a sea of blood trembles for me.

Oh still, closed garden that gives me
such a picture of peace, such
a longing for a calm
life at last, at last, at last serene!

But it is not to be, for
in the slightest breeze that rustles
the flowers and trees I hear
the roar of armored cars, a thundering
of death raining down from the heavens, from
all sides, a
long night of the wounded, bent
forever into the earth.

Sarebbe tanto bello starsene—quì—tranquilli,
il mondo in assoluta pace,
ascoltare questa fonte la mattina,
senza pensare che la sua pura, chiara voce
per me si frantuma in mille lamenti mentre scorre,
e un mare di sangue rabbrividisce
nei suoi domati fiotti.

Oh giardino conchiuso che mi offri una
simile imagine di pace, questo mio
anelito alla calma vita,
infine, infine, infine serena!

Ma non era destino, perchè
nella leggera brezza che accarezza
i fiori e gli alberi, io sento
il fragore di carri-armati, il tuono
di morte che si abbatte dal cielo,
in ogni angolo. La lunga
notte dei feriti, piegati
per sempre, verso il suolo.

nocturno

Toma y toma la llave de Roma,
porque en Roma hay una calle,
en la calle hay una casa,
en la casa hay una alcoba,
en la alcoba hay una cama,
en la cama hay una dama,

nocturne

Take, oh take the key to Rome,
for in Rome there's a street,
on the street there's a house,
in the house there's a room,
in the room there's a bed,
in the bed there's a damsel,

notturno

Porta e riporta la chiave di Roma,
in quanto a Roma esiste una via,
e nella via una casa,
e nella casa un'alcova,
e nell'alcova un letto,
e nel letto una signora,

una dama enamorada,	a damsel in love,	una signora innamorata,
que toma la llave,	who takes the key,	che porta la chiave,
que deja la cama,	who leaves the bed,	che lascia il letto,
que deja la alcoba,	who leaves the room,	che lascia l'alcova,
que deja la casa,	who leaves the house,	che lascia la casa,
que sale a la calle,	who goes out to the street,	che va nella strada,
que toma una espada,	who picks up a sword,	che prende una spada,
que corre en la noche,	who runs through the night,	che corre nella notte,
matando al que pasa,	killing someone who passes by,	uccidendo un passante,
que vuelve a su calle,	who goes back to her street,	che ritorna nella sua strada,
que vuelve a su casa,	who goes back to her house,	che ritorna nella sua casa,
que sube a su alcoba,	who goes up to her room,	che ritorna nella sua stanza,
que se entra en su cama,	who climbs into her bed,	che risale nel letto,
que esconde la llave,	who hides the key,	che nasconde la chiave,
que esconde la espada,	who hides the sword,	che nasconde la spada,
quedándose Roma	leaving Rome	lasciando Roma
sin gente que pasa,	without passersby,	con un passante in meno,
sin muerte y sin noche,	without death and without night,	senza morte e senza notte,
sin llave y sin dama.	without a key and without a damsel.	senza chiave e senza signora.

1
A Santa María
entran más que fieles
tristes aparatos
de fotografía.

2
Tres altos mascarones me miran por la boca,
muriéndose de risa por los ojos.

3
La forma de los senos y de los muslos,
el largo de los brazos,
la medida del talle y las caderas,
cuelgan de las ventanas y balcones
a la luna de mayo del Trastevere.

4
Huele a flores de acacia, a irresistibles,
blandos, hondos aromas seminales.

1
More pathetic photographic
gadgets
than worshippers
enter the Church of Santa Maria.

2
Three grotesque masks stare at me through their mouths,
dying of laughter through their eyes.

3
The shape of their breasts and thighs,
the length of their arms,
the size of their waist and hips,
hang from windows and balconies
under the May moon in the Trastevere.

4
It smells of acacia flowers, of irresistible,
soft, deep seminal aromas.

1
A Santa Maria
vi entrano più che fedeli
tristi apparati
di fotografia.

2
Là in alto tre mascheroni mi guardano attraverso la bocca,
morendo di risate attraverso gli occhi.

3
La forma del loro seno e cosce,
la lunghezza delle braccia,
la misura dei fianchi e delle anche,
pendono dalle finestre e balconi
sotto la luna di maggio di Trastevere.

4
Profumo di fiori di acacia, di irresistibile,
dolce, profondo aroma seminale.

5

Viejas enanas, tristes zarrapastros,
los pelos confundidos
con los colgajos de los trajes rotos.

6

Cuelgan de las esquinas las coronas
en honor de los héroes
mudos y vivos de la Resistencia.

7

Se ajan flores y lazos que circundan
los nombres de los héroes en las lápidas.
Mas todos allí siguen, permanecen,
como los fuertes muros que los alzan.

5

Shriveled old ladies in tattered rags,
their hair tangled
with the shreds of their torn clothing.

6

Wreaths hang from street corners
in honor of the silent,
living heroes of the Resistance.

7

The flowers and ribbons surrounding the names
of the heroes on their tombstones wither.
But they are all still there, as permanent
as the mighty walls that hold them aloft.

5

Piccole, vecchie donne, tristi stracci,
dai capelli mescolati
ai frammenti dei loro miseri indumenti.

6

Pendono dagli angoli le corone
in onore degli eroi
muti e viventi della Resistenza.

7

Sfiniscono i fiori e i nastri che circondano
i nomi degli eroi sulle lapide.
Ma sono ancora qui, ancora a resistere
come i forti muri che li sostengono.

tú no has llegado a roma para soñar

Tú no has llegado a Roma para soñar. Al cabo
de no sé cuánto tiempo, te preguntas: ¿Qué haces
rompiéndote los pies contra las piedras, yéndote
de pecho y de cabeza contra los muros, dándote
a todos los demonios por las sombras, royendo
tu propia vieja carne hasta llegar al punto
en que los huesos mondos aparecen al aire,
mientras que te devanas alrededor de ti,
sabiendo lo que esperas, aunque no llega nunca?
Tú no has llegado a Roma para soñar. Los sueños
se quedaron tan lejos, que ya ni los divisas,
ni ellos te buscan ya, pues ni te conocen.

you did not come to rome to dream

You did not come to Rome to dream. After
God knows how long, you ask yourself: Why
are you smashing your feet against the stones, careening
headfirst, hurtling your body into the walls, giving
yourself over to all the demons in the shadows, gnawing on
your own aged flesh until
your naked bones are exposed to the wind,
while you spool around yourself,
knowing what you're waiting for, though it will never arrive?
You did not come to Rome to dream. Your
dreams stayed far behind, so far you can no longer see them,
and they no longer seek you out, for they no longer know you.

non sei venuto a roma per sognare

Non sei venuto a Roma per sognare. Passato è,
Dio solo lo sa, tantissimo tempo, e ora ti chiedi: Perchè
ti struggi i piedi contro i sassi, correndo
a testa in giù, battendo petto e testa contro i muri, votandoti
a tutti i diavoli nelle ombre, rosicchiandoti la
tua vecchia carne fino a rivelare allo scoperto
le tue monde ossa,
mentre ti contorci a spirale su te stesso,
certo di quel che ti aspetti, sebbene mai arrivi?
Non sei venuto a Roma per sognare. I tuoi sogni
sono oramai così distanti che non riesci a scorgerli,
loro non ti seguono più, perchè non ti conoscono.

cuando me vaya de roma

A Ignazio Delogu

Cuando me vaya de Roma,
¿quién se acordará de mí?

Pregunten al gato,
pregunten al perro
y al roto zapato.

Al farol perdido,
al caballo muerto
y al balcón herido.

Al viento que pasa,
al portón oscuro
que no tiene casa.

Y al agua corriente
que escribe mi nombre
debajo del puente.

Cuando me vaya de Roma,
pregunten a ellos por mí.

when i leave rome

To Ignazio Delagu

When I leave Rome,
who will remember me?

Ask the cat,
ask the hound,
ask the boot that's worn to the ground.

The lamp that's lost,
the horse that tumbled,
the balconies that fell and crumbled.

The winds that roam,
the dark doorway
that has no home.

And the running stream
that writes my name
beneath the bridge's beam.

When I leave Rome,
ask them about me.

quando me ne andrò da roma

Per Ignazio Delagu

Quando me ne andrò via da Roma,
chi si ricorderà di me?

Domandatelo al gatto,
domandatelo al cane
ed allo scarpone rotto.

Alla lampada perduta,
al cavallo perito
e al balcone ferito.

Al vento che viaggia,
al portone buio
oramai senza spiaggia.

E all'acqua corrente
che scrive il mio nome
sotto i pilastri del ponte.

Quando me ne andrò via da Roma,
si domandi a tutti loro di me.

X

SONETOS

SONNETS

SONETTI

I

ya nada más…

Ya nada más entre tus sacros cantos
se oyen bocinas, pitos y sirenas,
y se ven por el cielo más antenas
que alas y palmas de ángeles y santos.

Ya por el Tíber no resbalan llantos
ni ya sus aguas rompen sus cadenas
y las Venus ya son menos obscenas
que un cardenal rendido a sus encantos.

Ya la invención de tu imaginería
bajó a morir en la bisutería
que los turistas de pasada abonan.

Mas las victorias de tus capiteles
aún alzan sus coronas de laureles…
de laureles que a nadie ya coronan.

now all you hear…

Now all you hear among your sacred chants
is honking horns, alarms, earsplitting whistles,
while reaching to the heavens antennas bristle,
displacing angels' wings and palms of saints.

No tears now flow along the Tiber's arms,
its waters do not break their chains pristine,
and the Venuses today are less obscene
than the cardinals in thrall to their great charms.

The inventions of your brilliant imagery
have shriveled up to die in cheap jewelry
in hopes that tourists might want to purchase some.

But the victories enshrined in your great capitals
still raise up high their sacred wreath of laurels…
a wreath of laurels today that crowns no one.

or non si ode che…

Or non si ode tra i tuoi sacri canti
altro che clacson, fischi e sirene,
e se ne van per il cielo più antenne
che ali e palme di angeli e di santi.

Sul Tevere non galleggian pianti,
nè le sue acque rompono catene
e le Veneri di sicuro meno oscene
di un cardinale sedotto dai suoi incanti.

L'imitazione di visi così belli
oggi scaduta è in bigiotteria
comprata da turisti di passaggio.

Ma le vittorie dei tuoi capitelli
alzan coron di lauro e checchessia
senza che il lauro conservi alcun retaggio.

II

gatos, gatos y gatos…

Gatos, gatos y gatos y más gatos
me cercaron la alcoba en que dormía.
Pero gato que entraba no salía,
muerto en las trampas de mis diez zapatos.

Cometí al fin tantos asesinatos,
que en toda Roma ningún gato había.
Mas la rata implantó su monarquía,
sometiendo al ratón a sus mandatos.

Y así hallé tal castigo, que no duermo,
helado, inmóvil, solo, mudo, enfermo,
viendo agujerearse los rincones,

condenado a morir viviendo a gatas,
en la noche comido por las ratas
y en el amanecer por los ratones.

cats, ten thousand cats...

Cats, ten thousand cats, and still more cats
laid siege to the lovely alcove where I sleep.
But any cat who entered found no escape
and died a bloody death as I laid traps.

At last my shoes committed so many murders
that not a single cat in Rome remained,
and then the rats imposed their sovereign reign,
subjecting all the mice to martial orders.

My punishment's ordained, I cannot sleep,
while frozen, still, alone, and mute I weep,
as all my walls relentlessly are gnawed,

while I'm condemned to crawl through all this blight,
devoured by raging hordes of rats at night
and marauding swarms of mice at break of dawn.

gatti, gatti e gatti…

Gatti, gatti, e gatti e ancora gatti
circondarono l'alcova in cui dormivo.
Ma ogni gatto che entrava stava lì furtivo,
morto restava fra i miei dieci scarponi sfatti.

Infine furon tanti i miei delitti,
che in tutta Roma non restaron più gatti.
E così i ratti presero il potere,
sottoponendo i topi al lor volere.

E quindi al non poter dormir son castigato,
malato, immobile, solo, muto, congelato,
guardando i tanti buchi aprirsi ad ogni lato,

condannato a morir vivendo inginocchiato,
nella notte dai topi divorato,
e dai ratti all'alba minacciato.

III

entro, señor, en tus iglesias…

Entro, señor, en tus iglesias… dime,
si tienes voz, ¿por qué siempre vacías?
Te lo pregunto por si no sabías
que ya a muy pocos tu pasión redime.

Respóndeme, señor, si te deprime
decirme lo que a nadie le dirías:
si entre las sombras de esas naves frías
tu corazón anonadado gime.

Confiésalo, señor, sólo tus fieles
hoy son esos anónimos tropeles
que en todo ven una lección de arte.

Miran acá, miran allá, asombrados,
ángeles, puertas, cúpulas, dorados…
y no te encuentran por ninguna parte.

i step, oh lord, into your sacred halls…

I step, oh Lord, into your sacred halls…
If you can speak, why is there no one here?
Please tell me. I ask in case you're unaware
that your passion today redeems so very few souls.

Answer, oh Lord, if this depresses you
and tell me what you would tell no one else:
If in these somber naves you yourself
feel your heart astonished, grieving and blue.

Confess, the only ones who worship here,
oh Lord, are the nameless hordes that draw near
and see here nothing but an art history lesson.

They look here, look there, and then, astonished, they falter,
at angels, doorways, gilt domes, magnificent altars…
and fail to find your soul or a single blessing.

entro, signore, nelle tue chiese…

Entro, Signore, nelle tue chiese… fammi capire,
se ti resta fiato, perchè sembran tutte un deserto?
Lo chiedo nel caso tu non ti fossi accorto
che solo pochi la tua passion può stupire.

Rispondimi, Signore, se ti fa patire
confidami ciò che a nessuno mai diresti:
se nelle ombre di queste navate fresche
il cuore tuo ancor continua a soffrire.

Confessalo, Signore. I tuoi fedeli
oggi son solo orde anonime i cui veli
lascian veder solo una lezione di arte.

Guardano qua, guardano là, meravigliati,
angeli, porte cupoloni dorati…
ma non ti incontrano da alcuna parte.

IV

artrosis (I)

¿Qué te sucede, que andas tan torcido,
a barquinazos por la Roma eterna,
sacando pierna o ya metiendo pierna,
perennemente de una tranca asido?

Que está tu cuerpo ya más que jodido,
se ve en que va como en corriente alterna,
pues se encuaderna o se desencuaderna,
pierniencogido o ya piernitendido.

Ojo avizor, no hay quien no esté pendiente
de contemplarte complacidamente
cuando en vaivén –un, dos, un, dos– paseas.

Y al fin del Campidoglio al Vaticano,
del Pincio a la Columna de Trajano...
Roma ya sabe de qué pie cojeas.

arthritis (I)

What's happened to you, your body's so twisted,
through Rome's eternal streets you lurch about,
your legs bend in and then fling wildly out,
while clutching a cane to keep from tilting and listing?

That your body is more than completely fucked up,
which is readily apparent like alternating current,
for it's bound and unbound in a rushing torrent,
your leg first stretched out and then plucked up.

Beware, for there's no one who's not keenly alert
to placidly watch as you lumber and lurch
as down the street you zigzag and weave.

And finally you limp from the Campidoglio to the Vatican,
from the Pincio to the towering column of Trajan...
All of Rome now watches and knows why you stumble and grieve.

artrosi (I)

Cosa ti succede, che ti riduce così attorcigliato,
barcamenarti per la Roma eterna,
buttando una gamba fuori o tirarla di lato,
perennemente ad una staffa aggrappato?

Che questo tuo corpo sia oramai fottuto,
è evidente perchè si muove a fase alterna,
poi si lega e si rilega a fase odierna,
gamba dentro gamba fuori come voluto.

Attenzione, tutti son lì ad aspettare
gioiosi di godersi il tuo ondulare
–uno, due, uno, due– al tuo passare.

E infine, zoppicante dal Campidoglio al Vaticano,
dal Pincio alla Colonna di Traiano...
tutta Roma guarda e sa perchè tu soffri e continui a zoppicare.

V

artrosis (II)

No puedo caminar, estoy más cojo
que el propio don Francisco de Quevedo.
Y el gran drama romano es que ni puedo
poner ya el pie en el Tíber al remojo.

Las piedras en las calles me dan miedo
y las siete colinas, mal de ojo.
¿Qué sería de mí si un toro rojo
escogiera mi barrio como ruedo?

Maldigo rampas, torres, escalones,
cúpulas, campaniles, murallones…
subir me rinde, descender me mata.

Y el ya no caminar tanto me cuesta,
que mi solemne conclusión es ésta:
no puedo en Roma ni estirar la pata.

arthritis (II)

I cannot walk, I'm even more hobbled and lame
than Don Francisco de Quevedo, the Golden Age poet.
And the great Roman tragedy as I intimately know it
is that now I can't dip my toes in the Tiber, to my shame.

The winding cobblestone streets inspire great fear,
and Rome's seven hills cast a cruel evil eye.
What's to become of me if a red bull should try
to charge in the alleys and squares of my quarter so dear?

I curse the ramps, the towers, the ubiquitous stairs,
the domes, belltowers, and the high walls, yet no one cares…
Climbing up is exhausting, walking down I flop like a puppet.

To be unable to walk is such a great challenge for me
that I've reached the solemn conclusion that all can see:
In Rome I won't even be able to kick the bucket.

artrosi (II)

Non posso camminar. Son più mal messo
di don Francisco de Quevedo.
E il grande dramma romano che prevedo
è che nel Tevere il piede bagnar non mi è concesso.

Le pietre dei vicoli con timor vedo
e ai sette colli guardo con occhio perplesso.
Cosa sarebbe di me se un toro rosso
scegliesse il mio vicinato per corredo?

Maledico rampe, scalinate, torrioni,
cupole, campanili e muraglioni…
ascenderli mi sconfigge, e discenderne mi è morte.

E non poter camminar tanto mi costa,
che la mia solenne conclusion è questa:
a Roma non posso neanche sfidar la sorte.

VI

*Tres nocturnos romanos
con don Ramón del Valle-Inclán*

*Three Roman nocturnes
with Don Ramón del Valle-Inclán*

*Tre notturni romani
con don Ramón del Valle-Inclán*

nocturno 1

Oigo llover tus barbas largamente
esta noche de Roma por lo oscuro,
de jardín en jardín, de muro en muro,
rotas columnas y de fuente en fuente.

Oigo tu voz de sátiro demente
y oigo tu solo brazo alzarse duro
contra esta noche, extraño sueño impuro
de un alma en pena que vagara ausente.

Oigo tu voz... te siento aquí a mi lado.
Voy en tus ciegas barbas enredado
como una insomne sombra clandestina,

y te sigo del Foro al Palatino,
del Gianicolo al Pincio, al Aventino
o a los Jardines de la Farnesina.

nocturne 1

I hear your long beard raining grizzled and solemn
tonight in Rome while blinded by impenetrable dark,
from wall to wall, and garden to closed garden,
from fountain to running fountain and broken columns.

I hear your satyr's voice cry out demented,
and I also hear you raise your one lone arm
to ward off this night, the strangest dream of harm
for a soul in limbo wandering lost and absent.

I hear your voice... I feel you here by my side.
I wander tangled in your blind beard and hide
while sleepless clandestine shadows close in and harden,

as I follow you from the Forum to the Palatino,
from the Gianicolo to the Pincio and the Aventino,
or stumble along with you to the Farnese gardens.

notturno 1

Sento piovigginare la tua barba possente
in questa notte romana in pieno oscuro,
di giardino in giardino, di muro in muro,
colonne rotte e fontana a fonte.

Sento la tua voce di satiro demente,
e sento il tuo solo braccio alzarsi duro
contro questa notte, strano sogno impuro
di un'anima in pena che vaga assente.

Sento la tua voce... ti sento qui al mio lato.
Nella tua folta barba ingarbugliato
come un insonne ombra clandestina,

e ti seguo dal Foro al Palatino,
dal Gianicolo al Pincio, all'Aventino,
fino ai Giardini della Farnesina.

VII

nocturno intermedio 2

Pasan cosas oscuras hoy: colmillos
hincados hasta el centro de las cejas,
virgos difuntos, calvas vulvas viejas,
desmelenados penes amarillos.

Bisoñés, bocios, gafas, lobanillos,
narices salpicadas de lentejas,
niños cangrejos, célibes almejas,
monjas garbanzos, frailes panecillos.

Pasan, pasan oscuras, sordamente,
cosas de gente y gente que no es gente,
bajo un sopor mordido de carcoma.

Tiempo es ya de volver para la casa,
porque no sé lo que esta noche pasa,
lo que esta noche está pasando en Roma.

intermediate nocturne 2

Dark things are happening here today: fangs
sunk deep and sharp between astonished eyes,
hymens defunct, as hairless vulvas cry,
while sorrowful yellow penises limply hang.

Eyeglasses, hairpieces, infected tumors and goiters,
mouths, faces and noses splattered with lentils,
celibate shellfish, crab children to peddle,
as garbanzo nuns and breadloaf monks still loiter.

Dark things, dark things are happening here today,
dark human things to drive the humans away,
in a worm-eaten stupor that none are able to fight.

It's well past time for us to go back home,
for I do not know what's happening now in Rome,
I do not know what's happening here tonight.

notturno intermedio 2

Oggi accadono tenebrose cose: zanne
conficcate in mezzo agli occhi,
vergini defunte, tenaci vulve a spicchi,
peni ingialliti e ormai senza più penne.

Parrucche, gozzi, vetri, vesciche,
narici mantecate con lenticchie,
granchi fanciulli, vongole illibate,
suore ai ceci, e frati impanati.

Accadono cose tenebrose, accadono, sordamente,
cose di gente e gente che non è gente,
in un sopor mordicchiato da un tarlo.

È giunta l'ora di far ritorno a casa,
perchè stanotte sta accadendo non so cosa,
in questa notte che sta passando a Roma.

VIII

nocturno 3

Te hablo aquí desde Roma, dios endriago,
hoy por tan malas manos mal traído,
trasgo zumbón, demonio aborrecido,
chula navaja, rústico zurriago.

Clava tu luz en mi nocturno aciago,
afila mi colmillo retorcido
y no me dejes cariacontecido
a la mitad de tan amargo trago.

Yaces tú allí, yo aquí, aún en destierro,
gato en la noche y por el día perro,
solo bajo esta lápida romana.

Deja al fin tu galaica sepultura
y ven conmigo en esta noche oscura
a esperar cómo sube la mañana.

nocturne 3

I speak to you here in Rome, oh monstrous god,
today when malicious hands have taken their toll
on you, detested demon, wicked trickster troll,
you lowlife blade, you rustic cattle prod.

Now shine your brightest light on my ill-fated verse
and sharpen my twisted fangs with your very best tool,
don't leave me alone and crestfallen to look like a fool
when I'm only halfway through this terrible curse.

There lie you, and here lie I, in exile,
a barking dog by day, a cat by night,
as I lie by myself beneath this Roman tombstone.

Abandon at last your grave, for this is our trial,
and walk with me into this deep dark night
to wait and see the morning rise alone.

notturno 3

Ti parlo da Roma, dio dragone,
oggi da tante cattive mani mal trattato,
sfottente diavoletto, bizzoso e indemoniato,
lama di magnaccio, colpo da coglione.

Irrora la tua luce sul mio notturno profetizzante,
affila la mia malefica zanna uncinata,
e salvami da ogn'apparenza instupidita,
appena a metà di questo amaro calice bruciante.

Tu giaci lì, io qui, ancora esiliato,
gatto di notte, e giorno cane arrabbiato,
sta solo sotto questa lapide romana.

Esci dalla tua galiziana sepoltura
e accompagnami in questa notte oscura
ad aspettar il salir dell'alba urbana.

IX

respuesta del tiempo

A Bertolt Brecht

Hoy mis ojos se han vuelto navegantes
de los profundos cielos estrellados.
Miran y ven pasar maravillados
los terrestres satélites errantes.

Nacidos de los hombres, trajinantes
obedientes a todos sus mandatos,
son para los espacios desvelados
los caballeros de la luz andantes.

Así, regidos, cumplen las alturas
y las más rigurosas aventuras,
según le impulse el hombre su deseo.

Y en las romanas noches de verano,
se les siente reír del Vaticano
que hundió en la noche oscura a Galileo.

time's answer

To Bertolt Brecht

Today my eyes have learned to navigate
the deepest, darkest distant starlit skies.
They gaze in wonder as they see flying by
the terrestrial wandering satellites.

Born of man, they soar in sonic flight
as they obey his each and every order,
they are in sleepless space that knows no borders,
the noble knights errant of the universe of light.

And thus commanded they reach the greatest heights
through the most demanding and adventurous flights,
impelled by man's insatiable desire to explore.

And in the sensual Roman summer nights
you hear laughter rise above the Vatican's lights
that sank Galileo in the tragic silence he bore.

risposta del tempo

per Bertold Brecht

Oggi i miei occhi son vele diventati
dei profondi universi stellati.
Guardan e vedon passar meravigliati
i terrestri satélliti dorati.

Da umani nati, trainanti
obedienti and ogni suo volere,
sono per gli spazi risvegliati
della luce i cavalieri erranti.

Così, governati, raggiungon le alture
e le più rigorose avventure,
seguendo l'impulso e desiderio umano.

E nella romana notte di calure,
del Vatican li si sente rider pure
che affondò Galileo tempo lontano.

X

oyes correr en roma…

Oyes correr en Roma eternamente,
en la noche, en el día, a toda hora,
el agua, el agua, el agua corredora
de una fuente, otra fuente y otra fuente.

Arrebatada acústica demente,
infinita insistencia corredora,
cante en lo oscuro, gima bullidora,
es su fija locura ser corriente.

Ría de un ojo, llore de unos senos,
salte de un caracol, de entre la boca
de la más afilada dentadura

o de las ingles de unos muslos llenos,
correrá siempre desmandada y loca,
libre y presa y perdida en su locura.

you hear in rome…

You hear in Rome eternally bubbling and flowing,
all night, all day, always running, forever,
water, water, water that never stops, never,
from one fountain, from another, never slowing.

Eternal anarchic acoustic insanity,
infinite internal insistence on constantly running,
it sings in the dark and moans and groans while burbling,
the endless madness to always run is its vanity.

It laughs through an eye, it weeps from stone breasts,
it bursts from a snail, it spews from pursed lips
that conceal the sharpest set of vicious teeth

or from the loins of sensuous thighs undressed,
it always, uncontrolled, gushes and drips,
free and restrained and lost in its mad belief.

si sente correre a roma…

A Roma si sente correre da ponte a ponte,
la notte, il giorno, ad ogni ora,
l'acqua, l'acqua, l'acqua che ancora
scorre da una fonte, altra fonte e altra fonte.

Incontrollata acustica demente,
infinita insistenza corritrice,
canta nel buio, gemi bollitrice,
e la sua fissa follia esser corrente.

Ridi da un occhio, da un seno lacrima esce,
salta da una lumaca, penetra le labbra molle
della più affilata dentatura

o degli inguini di piene cosce,
correrà per sempre sbrigliata e folle,
libera, prigioniera e smarrita nella sua paura.

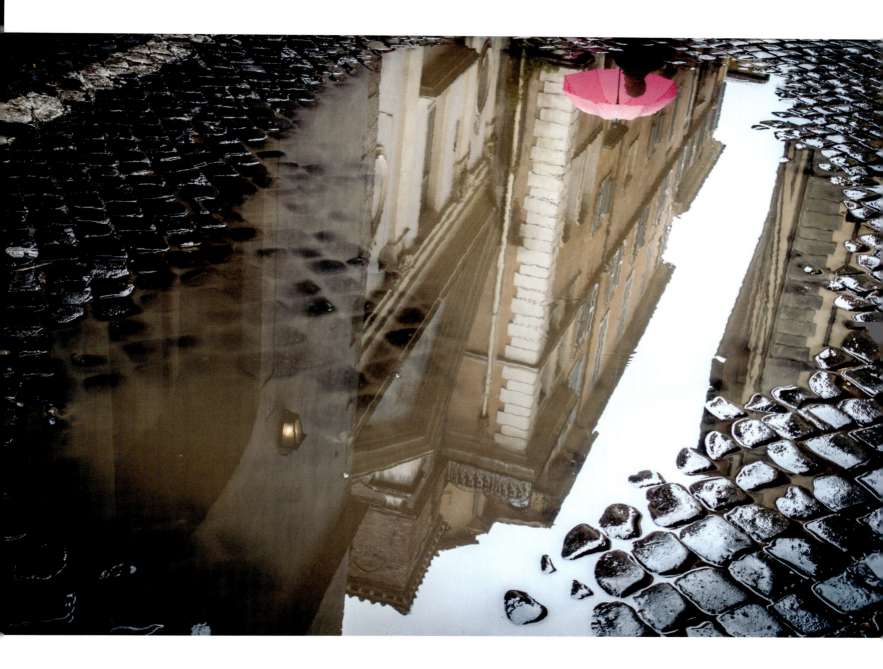

Apéndice
Appendix
Appendice

Rafael Alberti en Roma / Roma en Rafael Alberti

Anthony L. Geist

Rafael Alberti nace y muere con el siglo xx. Ve la luz por primera vez en El Puerto de Santa María (Cádiz, España) en 1902 y allí fallece en 1999, cerrando el círculo. Miembro de la mítica Generación del 27, Alberti fue un poeta prolífico, publicando más de treinta libros de poesía. Su poesía nace bajo el signo de la nostalgia, nostalgia de aquello que ha tenido que dejar atrás, pues su vida es una serie de sucesivos exilios. Sufre el primer exilio a los quince años cuando su padre traslada a la familia de la Bahía de Cádiz a Madrid en 1917. Al final de la guerra civil en 1939, con su mujer María Teresa León, se escapa de España a Orán y de allí a París, donde viven con Pablo Neruda y Delia del Carril. Pero ese refugio solo dura un año, pues con la ocupación nazi de la capital francesa en 1940 tienen que huir nuevamente, esta vez a Argentina, donde viven hasta 1963, cuando se ven obligados a abandonar el país por un gobierno peronista de derechas. Deciden volver a Europa, estableciéndose en Roma, capital del país ancestral de los Alberti.

Es allí, entre 1964 y 1967, donde escribe Alberti *Roma, peligro para caminantes* (1968), libro que recoge la impresión que le hizo la ciudad. Los poemas expresan el caos, el tráfico, la inmundicia, meadas, mojones, ropa tendida, gatos y ratones, pícaros, multitudes en las calles, junto con la vitalidad, la gloria de los monumentos, ruinas imperiales, iglesias, fuentes y jardines de la *Città Eterna*. Esa "basura" no se opone a la gloria imperial de Roma, sino que dependen precisamente una de otra.

Roma, peligro para caminantes es polifacético y muy cuidadosamente organizado. Arranca con "Monserrato, 20", un largo poema en endecasílabos blancos donde el hablante desciende de su casa y entra en Roma, en lo que un crítico entiende como una penetración y unión sexual con la ciudad.[*] Dos suites de sonetos abren y cierran el libro y entremedio Alberti despliega con maestría poemas en verso libre, heptasílabos y octosílabos rimados. Algunos de los temas principales que vertebran el libro incluyen la inmundicia, la escatología, poemas escénicos, nocturnos, la hermosura y la nostalgia.

Vemos representaciones de la inmundicia en varios poemas pero donde más se destaca es en "Cuando Roma es…" donde una acumulación caótica de imágenes negativas de la ciudad ("cloaca, / mazmorra, calabozo, / catacumba, cisterna / […] / mares de ácido úrico, / bocanadas de muertos") lleva a los versos finales que parecieran plantear una contradicción: "entonces, oh, sí, entonces, / sueña en los pinos, sueña". Sin embargo, sentir profundamente los hedores es precisamente lo que lleva al poeta a soñar entre los pinos del Gianicolo, la segunda colina más alta de Roma.

Una parte destacada de la inmundicia que llama la atención de Alberti, y que figura de manera importante en varios poemas, es la escatología. Abundan meadas y mojones, casi siempre en clave irónica y humorística. Donde se explaya más la escatología es en varios poemas dedicados a la micción, desde el soneto III, "Se prohíbe hacer aguas", hasta la serie de trece breves poemas

---

[*] Juan Carlos Rodríguez, "Un modo de lectura textual (Para un análisis de la poética de Alberti a través de un soneto de *Roma*)," *Nueva Estafeta* 53 (Abril 1983): 35–45.

bajo el título colectivo de "Todavía tocante a las meadas", donde declara "¡Oh ciudad mingitorio del Universo! Eres / la única capital reconocida / de todas las meadas".

A lo largo de *Roma, peligro para caminantes* Alberti incluye cinco textos que define como "poemas escénicos". Como su nombre implica son pequeñas obras teatrales, con personajes y protagonistas claramente definidos (en algún caso el propio poeta forma parte del elenco) y con diálogo entre ellos. En "Diálogo mudo con un vecino" el poeta reprocha al vecino por haberle meado los zapatos:

> […] Tu meada
> me persiguió como una larga lengua
> hasta mojarme los zapatos… Luego,
> sin importarte un rábano, pasaste
> silbando junto a mí…

El diálogo es mudo porque solo escuchamos las palabras del vecino a través de las respuestas del hablante.

Hay ocho nocturnos a lo largo de *Roma*, todos con el mismo título, 'Nocturno". En general comparten una oscuridad no solo nocturna sino espiritual o psicológica. En uno se niega a nombrar un ser, o quizás el recuerdo de un evento traumático personificado, que lo persigue: "La otra noche vi… / ¿A quién vi?" Otros nocturnos expresan una profunda soledad: "De pronto, Roma está sola, / Roma está sola, sin nadie". En los nocturnos vemos otro lado de Roma, el lado oscuro, ominoso.

Si el caos y la basura coexisten con los sueños, de la misma manera que conviven lo material y lo espiritual, también reside la hermosura al lado de la miseria en otros poemas de *Roma, peligro para caminantes*. "Invitación para el mes de agosto", por ejemplo, representa la sensualidad veraniega de las fuentes de Roma: "¡Fuentes que sin disimulo / bañan en agua a las ninfas / desde las tetas al culo!" La luminosidad de estos versos reside no solo en la sexualidad de los cuerpos desnudos sino también en las rimas consonantes. La aparente contradicción entre la oscuridad en algunos poemas con la alegría aquí presente no significa que sean contrarios. Sin la oscuridad no hay luz, y sin la luminosidad no hay oscuridad.

Roma, peligro para caminantes es una obra de nostalgia. La *nostalgia* se caracteriza por la añoranza del pasado. Es una palabra de origen culto, compuesta de dos palabras griegas: *nóstos* (la vuelta al hogar), palabra homérica, y *álgos* (dolor). Es precisamente el deseo de la vuelta al sitio de origen, y el dolor que provoca, lo que motiva un buen número de estos poemas. Donde lo expresa Alberti de forma más conmovedora es en el primer soneto que abre *Roma*, "Lo que dejé por ti", que concluye así:

> Dejé por ti todo lo que era mío.
> Dame tú, Roma, a cambio de mis penas,
> tanto como dejé para tenerte.

Vengan a pasear por las calles y los callejones de Roma de la mano y pluma de Rafael Alberti, en español, inglés e italiano, acompañados de las fotos de Adam Weintraub que dialogan con los poemas, pues "ésta en Roma es la vida de un poeta".

Rafael Alberti a Roma / Roma a Rafael Alberti

Anthony L. Geist

La vita di Rafael Alberti è iniziata e si è conclusa nel e con il ventesimo secolo. Ha dischiuso gli occhi per la prima volta a Puerto de Santa María (Cadige, Spagna) nel 1902, e si è spento nello stesso posto nel 1999, così chiudendo il cerchio della sua esistenza. Rafael Alberti fu un rappresentante di rilievo della mitica Generazione del '27, ed è stato un prolifico poeta, pubblicando più di trenta raccolte di poesie. La sua produzione poetica è segnata dalla nostalgia; un sentimento profondo di nostalgia per tutto ciò che era stato costretto a lasciarsi dietro, in quanto la sua esistenza si è risolta nel continuo esilio in vari paesi. Il primo esilio ha luogo all'età di quindici anni quando il padre trasferì la famiglia dalla baia di Cadige a Madrid nel 1917. Alla conclusione della Guerra Civile Spagnola nel 1939, insieme alla moglie María Teresa León, scapparono dalla Spagna per Oran (Algeria), e da lì si trasferirono a Parigi, dove condivisero casa con Pablo Neruda e Delia del Carril. Questo periodo fu molto breve, dura circa un anno, in quanto con l'invasione nazista della capitale francese nel 1940, furono costretti a fuggire nuovamente, questa volta in Argentina, dove vi vissero fino al 1963, fino a quando costretti a scappare per l'ennesima volta dal regime Peronista al momento al governo del paese. Così decisero di stabilirsi a Roma, la capitale della terra dei suoi antenati.

Ed è proprio lì, fra il 1964 e 1967, che Alberti scrisse *Roma, pericolo per i viandanti* (1968), un'opera in cui si racchiudono tutte le impressioni-emozioni che la città gli ha offerti e che ha avuto su di lui. Le liriche dipingono: caos, traffico, sporcizia di ogni fattura, rigagnoli di urina, cumuli di escrementi, panni appesi dai balconi e finestre, gatti e ratti, furfanti di ogni genere, le vie affollate,

tutto un mondo colmo di vitalità, la gloria dei suoi monumenti, rovine imperiali, chiese, fontane e giardini della Città Eterna. "L'immondizia" non sminuisce la gloria imperiale di Roma, anzi, l'una dipende esattamente dall'altra.

Roma, pericolo per i viandanti è un'opera multiforme ed attentamente organizzata. L'opera si apre con la lirica "Monserrato, 20", un componimento scritto in undici sillabe in versi sciolti in cui la voce poetica scende le scale della sua casa per entrare nel cuore del vicinato e quindi Roma, al punto che un critico lo interpreta come una penetrazione sessuale ed unione con la città.[*] Due serie di sonetti aprono e chiudono la raccolta fungendone da cornice in cui Alberti colloca magistrali liriche in verso libero che si alternano a versi misurati e rimati. Alcune delle tematiche ricorrenti nell'ambito della struttura includono sporcizia, immagini scatologiche, poesie drammatiche, notturni, bellezza e nostalgia.

Nel complesso della raccolta sono numerose le liriche caratterizzate da immagini di sporcizia, ma dove questo elemento appare prevalente è la poesia "Quando Roma è…" in cui si accumula in modo caotico ogni possibile immagine negativa della città ("cloaca, / gattabuia, carcere, / catacomba, cisterna / [...] / mari di acido urico / boccate di morti") conducono ai versi conclusivi che sembrano contraddire quello affermato precedentemente: "quindi, oh, sì, quindi, / sogna i tuoi pini, sogna." Ma il vivere l'esperienza del fetore e della

---

[*] Juan Carlos Rodríguez, "Un modo de lectura textual (Para un análisis de la poética de Alberti a través de un soneto de *Roma*)," *Nueva Estafeta* 53 (Aprile 1983): 35–45.

sporcizia è esattamente ciò che permette all'autore di sognare sotto i pini del Gianicolo, la seconda più alta collina di Roma.

La maggior parte della sporcizia che coglie l'attenzione dell'autore e che ha un ruolo prominente nella raccolta *Roma, pericolo per i viandanti*, è scatologica. In tante liriche noi vediamo urina e feci, quasi sempre raccontate in un tono di ironia e umore. La scatologia è prevalentemente ovvia nelle liriche dedicate all'urina, dal sonetto III, "Si proibisce pisciare", alla serie di tredici liriche sotto il titolo "Sempre a riguardo del pisciare", in cui il poeta afferma: "Oh città orinatoio dell'Universo! Sei / unicamente riconosciuta la capitale / di tutte le pisciate."

Sparsi all'interno della raccolta *Roma, pericolo per i viandanti* l'autore include cinque liriche che definisce come "poesie drammatiche". Come facilmente deducibile dal titolo che Alberti attribuisce a questo gruppo di liriche, sono costituite da piccole scene teatrali con personaggi e protagonisti chiaramente definiti, e i relativi dialoghi fra loro in cui, di tanto in tanto, l'autore stesso si inserisce nel cast di questi personaggi. In "Dialogo muto con un vicino", il poeta rimprovera il suo vicino per avergli pisciato sulle scarpe:

> […] La tua pisciata
> mi inseguì come una lunga lingua
> ad inzupparmi le scarpe… Poi,
> ignorando il tutto, fischiettante
> mi sei passato vicino…

Il dialogo è silente inquanto noi sentiamo le parole del vicino solo attraverso la risposta della voce poetica.

In *Roma, pericolo per i viandanti* sono inclusi otto notturni: tutti portano l'identico titolo: "Notturno". In generale condividono un'oscurità non solo notturna ma anche spirituale, psicologica, metafisica. In uno dei notturni il poeta rifiuta di riconoscere un essere, o forse la memoria di un personificato even-

to traumatico che lo persegue: "L'altra notte ho visto… / Chi ho visto?" Altri notturni esprimono profonda solitudine: "D'improvviso Roma è sola, / Roma è sola, senza nessuno". Nei notturni si intravede l'altro lato di Roma, quello oscuro, più minaccioso.

Se è possibile che caos e sporcizia possono coesistere coi sogni, così anche la materialità e la spiritualità possono condividere la vita fianco a fianco, in altre liriche la bellezza risiede accanto al dolore e alla sofferenza. "Invito per il mese di agosto" rappresenta la sensualità delle fontane di Roma: "Fontane che senza pudore alcuno / bagnan nelle loro acque le ninfe / dalle tette al culo!" La luminosità di questi versi risiede non soltanto nella sensualità dei nudi corpi ma anche nelle rime. L'apparente contraddizione fra l'oscurità di altre liriche con la giocosità dei versi su menzionati non necessariamente significa incompatibilità. Senza oscurità non esiste luce, e senza luce non c'è oscurità.

Come accennato in precedenza, *Roma, pericolo per i viandanti* è un'opera nata sotto il segno della nostalgia. Un desiderio per il passato è caratteristico della nostalgia. Il termine ha origini classiche e si compone di due parole in greco antico: *nóstos* (ritorno a casa) con toni omerici, ed *álgos* (dolore). Ed è esattamente il desiderio del ritorno al punto di origine con il relativo dolore che il ritorno causa che diventa motore di queste liriche. La poesia in cui Alberti riesce ad esprimere tutto questo è "Quel che lasciai per te", il sonetto che apre *Roma*, che si chiude con questa terzina:

> Per te lasciai ogni aver mio.
> Or dammi tu, Roma, al posto delle pene,
> tanto quanto ho lasciato per averti.

Ora, prendiamo la mano di Alberti e avviamoci per le vie di Roma, in spagnolo, inglese e italiano, dove le immagini di Adam Weintraub dialogano con le poesie, "Questa è la vita di un poeta a Roma".

Alberti, peligro para traductores
Anthony L. Geist y Giuseppe Leporace

Desciendo la escalera de mi casa,
mirado de relieves. ¿Dónde sueño?
Dioses del mar y atletas coronados,
cabezas de guerreros, bailarinas
cimbreadas de finos tallos ágiles...

"Monserrato, 20", el poema que abre *Roma, peligro para caminantes*, arranca con estos versos de movimiento físico literal. Alberti quiere tomar al lector de la mano y llevarnos, paso a paso, por un mundo de imágenes míticas. Despacio, a cada paso encontramos nuevos y fascinantes personajes. Al bajar los tres tramos de escaleras atravesamos el patio interior, salimos por el gigantesco portón del edificio renacentista y nos encontramos en la calle, ¡Via Monserrato 20! Escasos minutos antes estábamos rodeados de figuras mitológicas, dioses, guerreros clásicos, protagonistas ejemplares de los sentimientos y pasiones humanas de los que se compone "la naturaleza humana", en un universo de penumbra, enmudecidos en el silencio más absoluto, y de repente afuera, bajo el relumbrante sol, ahora al descubierto, sin protección, nos asalta el ruido de la calle, las voces de todos los "caminantes", el rugido de los motores de las Vespas y los FIAT 500. Y estamos perplejos, preguntándonos, como lo hizo Alberti: ¿Dónde sueño?

Ni se dan entrevistas ni se escriben prólogos

Estas palabras, en elegante caligrafía en español e italiano, esperaban a Geist cuando llamó a la puerta en la segunda planta del palazzo en la Via Garibaldi 88. Llevaba una carta de presentación y dos botellas de Jumilla de parte de D. Fulgencio Díaz Pastor para Rafael Alberti. Fue la primavera de 1972.

Alberti recibió a Geist sentado a una mesa en la entrada. Lo tuvo de pie interrogándole durante diez minutos antes de invitarle a pasar y tomar una copa de Fundador. Le explicó que a raíz del caso Padilla en Cuba quería asegurarse de que no era *agent provocateur*. Estuvieron más de dos horas conversando y Geist se fue eufórico, con un ejemplar de la edición de Aguilar de la poesía completa dedicado con un icónico dibujo.

Fue entonces cuando Geist empezó a leer *Roma, peligro para caminantes*, cautivado por la elegancia de los sonetos que abren y cierran el libro en yuxtaposición con las coplas y poemas en verso libre dedicados a temas tan variados como el excremento y la orina, la inmundicia, gatos y ratones, prostitutas y pícaros, ruinas imperiales y multitudes de turistas, teñidos con la nostalgia de aquello que tuvo que abandonar en sus sucesivos exilios.

Cuando Roma es cloaca,
Mazmorra, calabozo,
catacumba, cisterna,
albañal, inmundicias

[…]

entonces, oh, sí, entonces,

sueña en los pinos, sueña.

Los poemas de *Roma, peligro para caminantes* se centran en varios lugares icónicos de las áreas históricas de Roma: la presencia innegable del río Tíber, el Trastévere con su majestuosa iglesia de Santa María, el Campo de' Fiori donde confluyen las callejuelas atiborradas de tiendas de artesanía, los colores y olores de verduras y panes recién salidos del horno se mezclan con el hedor de orina en cada rincón de los callejones. Esta flora y fauna son los elementos básicos y la esencia que animan los poemas de Alberti.

Un día varios años después, tomando un café en la Universidad de Washington, nos reunimos—Geist y Leporace—para hablar de Alberti y su extraordinario poemario sobre Roma. Este proyecto conjunto nació de esas conversaciones. El proyecto se gestó de las múltiples conversaciones en que Geist compartió su conocimiento de la vida y obra del poeta. El interés y curiosidad de Leporace aumentaron y a su vez generaron más conversaciones, que desembocaron en la organización de un programa de estudios que se realizaría durante cuatro semanas en España e Italia. Por tanto, decidimos que la mejor aula para nuestro cometido serían las propias calles que describe el poeta gaditano. Leímos y analizamos los poemas en los lugares mismos que describen. Para todos ¡fue una experiencia mágica, sublime!

Nos reunimos con los estudiantes en Madrid, donde durante varios días exploramos la ciudad, su fabuloso Museo del Prado y otros sitios donde Alberti pasó parte de su vida antes de tener que huir de Franco y dejar España para las Américas, aterrizando finalmente en Roma, donde vivió casi veinte años.

De Madrid fuimos en tren a Cádiz, al otro lado de la bahía del Puerto de Santa María donde nació y se crió Alberti. Durante dos semanas en España rastreamos a Alberti desde su lugar de nacimiento hacia las distintas fases de su consolidación intelectual como español y poeta. Este segmento fue una experiencia extraordinaria para todo el grupo, con la culminación en Roma.

Varios años después, cuando decidimos traducir formalmente aquello que iniciamos con nuestros alumnos, se nos ocurrió que el complemento perfecto a la edición trilingüe sería un elemento visual. Geist me presentó a su amigo, el renombrado fotógrafo Adam Weintraub. En seguida Adam entendió el proyecto y lo acogió con entusiasmo. Conocía Roma pero quería familiarizarse con los sitios donde Alberti ambientó sus poemas. Necesitaba un Virgilio para guiarlo, primero por los poemas y luego por los lugares físicos, y yo fui su Virgilio. En Roma un bar en el Trastévere fue nuestro centro de investigación. Por la mañana repasamos los poemas para que Adam fuera entendiendo los contenidos precisos, la musicalidad y el ritmo de los versos, y luego pasamos a la acción, día y noche. Qué experiencia más trasformadora fue para mí entender cómo funciona la mente y el ojo de un fotógrafo. Indudablemente me ayudó a encontrar nuevas herramientas en mi propio empeño en traducir Roma, peligro para caminantes.

Giuseppe Leporace

No me podía imaginar que aquel primer encuentro en Roma sería el inicio de una larga amistad. En abril de 1981 invité a Alberti a un simposio en Dartmouth College sobre arte y literatura de la guerra civil. Allí fue, inspirado por mi estatura y mis melenas, que me apodó el "Rey de los Merovingios". Al año siguiente lo llevé a Granada donde pasó una memorable semana en mi piso. Varios dibujos que me hizo cuelgan hoy en las paredes de mi despacho y casa. Dio un recital ante un público masivo en el patio del Palacio de Puentezuelas donde leyó su poema dedicado a Federico García Lorca, "Balada del que nunca fue a Granada". Nos llevaron al barranco de Víznar para llorar la muerte de Lorca, asesinado por los fascistas insurrectos.

A lo largo de los años 80 y 90 cada vez que iba a Madrid o El Puerto quedaba con él. Lo vi por última vez un par de años antes de su muerte.

Anthony L. Geist

Alberti, pericolo per i traduttori
Anthony L. Geist e Giuseppe Leporace

Discendo le scale della mia nuova casa
scrutato da bassorilievi. Sto sognando?
Dei del mare e atleti incoronati,
teste di guerrieri, danzatrici
svolazzanti coperte di veli leggeri...

"Monserrato, 20", la poesia che apre la raccolta *Roma, pericolo per i viandanti*, inizia con questi versi che esprimono puro movimento fisico. In essi Alberti invita il lettore, tenendolo per mano, a seguirlo, passo dopo passo, in un mondo rappresentato attraverso immagini mitiche. E, man mano che scendiamo le scale, entriamo in contatto con altri affascinanti personaggi che da secoli abitano quei muri. Terminate le tre rampe di scale, attraversiamo il cortile, oltrepassiamo il gigantesco portone del palazzo rinascimentale per essere improvvisamente catapultati fuori, nella strada: Via Monserrato 20! Attimi prima eravamo raccolti nel caldo abbraccio di figure mitologiche: dei, guerrieri di un mondo lontano, di tanti protagonisti dei sentimenti e passioni umane che contraddistinguono la nostra "Natura". Eravamo in universo di ombra, ovattato da un silenzio assoluto, e all'improvviso ci siamo trovati fuori, accecati dalla violenta luce del sole, allo scoperto, senza protezione alcuna. Una volta all'esterno, come se quell'incantesimo fosse stato spezzato, siamo assaliti dall'assordante rumore della realtà della strada; dal vociare incessante dei "passanti"; torturati dal ruggito dei motori delle Vespa e Fiat 500! E d'improvviso siamo tutti in uno stato di sospensione—come immaginiamo sia successo ad Alberti ogni giorno; e ognuno dentro se stesso si chiede: "Sto sognando?"

Non si danno interviste, né si scrivono prologhi.

Queste sono le testuali parole in spagnolo e italiano, chiosate a mano in elegante calligrafia, che salutano Geist quando bussò alla porta del secondo piano del palazzo in Via Garibaldi 88, residenza di Rafael Alberti a Roma. Geist era accompagnato da una lettera di presentazione e due bottiglie di Jumilla da parte di D. Fulgencio Diaz Pastor. Siamo nella primavera del 1972.

Ad accoglierlo, seduto ad un tavolino nell'atrio della saletta d'ingresso c'era Alberti. Per circa dieci minuti, il padrone di casa lo sottopose e un intenso interrogatorio prima di invitarlo ad entrare in casa e condividere un bicchierino del suo Fundador. Alberti, una volta rotto il momento di ghiaccio, giustificò il suo atteggiamento di iniziale diffidenza, dicendo che voleva accertarsi che Geist non fosse un altro agente provocatore sulla scia del caso Padilla a Cuba. I due chiacchierarono piacevolmente per varie ore, e quando per Geist si fece l'ora di andare si sentiva come in uno stato di estasi, in quanto Alberti gli aveva fatto dono di una copia dell'edizione completa della sua opera poetica, autografata con un suo iconico disegno.

Fu allora che Geist iniziò a leggere *Roma, pericolo per i viandanti*, restando ammaliato dall'eleganza dei sonetti che aprono e chiudono la raccolta in giustapposizione con le liriche composte da distici e versi sciolti concentrati su tematiche che variano da escrementi e urina, a sporcizia, da gatti e ratti, a prostitute e criminali di basso rango, da rovine di epoca imperiale a mandrie

di turisti. Un universo che appariva spesso intinto di nostalgia per tutto ciò che Alberti si era lasciato dietro in ogni suo esilio.

> Quando Roma è cloaca,
> gattabuia, carcere,
> catacomba, cisterna,
> latrina, immondezzaio,
> [...]
> quindi, oh, sì, quindi,
> sogna i tuoi pini, sogna.

Le liriche in *Roma, pericolo per i viandanti* sono incentrate su luoghi simbolo dell'aria storica del centro di Roma: l'onnipresenza del Tevere; il brulichio di Trastevere con la sua maestosa chiesa di Santa Maria; Piazza Campo de' Fiori, in cui a matassa confluiscono stradine e vicoli pullulanti di piccoli negozi di artigianeria, con le botteghe emananti freschi profumi di fiori e frutti di orto appena raccolti o di pane appena sfornato, combinati al fetore di urina che esala in ogni angolo della strada. Questa flora e fauna romana sono gli ingredienti di base e l'essenza che animano le liriche di Alberti.

Gli anni passarono, e un giorno, mentre gustavamo un caffè nella caffetteria dell'Università di Washington, noi—Geist e Leporace—ci ritrovammo a discutere di Rafael Alberti e della sua straordinaria raccolta di poesie su Roma. Questo progetto di collaborazione ha la sua origine proprio da quelle conversazioni durante le quali Geist condivise la sua personale conoscenza del poeta e la sua produzione intellettuale. La condivisione di queste informazioni contribuì a stimolare la curiosità di Leporace per Alberti, e discusse e fatte le considerazioni necessarie, i due decisero di organizzare un programma di studi della durata di quattro settimane, due in Spagna e due a Roma. Per la parte riguardante il periodo a Roma, decidemmo, senza alcuna esitazione, che l'aula ideale per il seminario sarebbero state le strade e i luoghi descritti da Alberti nelle sue liriche. Alla fine, questo esperimento si dimostrò un'esperienza magica ed emotivamente coinvolgente per l'intero gruppo.

Incontrammo gli studenti a Madrid, dove trascorremmo alcuni giorni a esplorare la città, il suo favoloso Museo del Prado, e ogni altro luogo possibile in cui potevamo rintracciarvi la presenza di Alberti prima di essere costretto da Franco a lasciare la Spagna per le Americhe, per poi chiudere il cerchio degli anni di esilio a Roma, dove visse per quasi venti anni.

Da Madrid salimmo su un treno diretto a Cadige, cittadina situata sul lato opposto alla baia di El Puerto de Santa Maria dove Alberti era nato e cresciuto. Per la durata delle due settimane in Spagna, abbiamo seguito le tracce di Alberti dal suo paesino natale e per tutto il suo percorso di crescita intellettuale di uomo di Spagna e di poeta. Questo segmento si rivelò fantastico per il gruppo in preparazione della nostra culminante esperienza romana.

Anni dopo, quando abbiamo deciso di rielaborare e tradurre di tutto punto il lavoro iniziato insieme agli studenti, abbiamo concluso che eventuale pubblicazione di questa traduzione trilingue, per le sue peculiarità intrinseche, sarebbe stata ben complementata e sostenuta dall'aggiunta di elementi visivi. Immediatamente, Geist mi ha fatto conoscere un suo amico, il quale era un fotografo professionista già molto affermato, Adam Weintraub. Adam, dopo alcune piacevoli chiacchierate, comprese perfettamente lo spirito del progetto, e acconsentì con grande entusiasmo a questa collaborazione. Aveva precedentemente visitato Roma in varie occasioni, ma questa volta era per un motivo speciale che richiedeva qualcosa di più: aveva bisogno di visualizzare attraverso le poesie i luoghi che avevano funzionato da palcoscenico alle creazioni di Alberti. Per ottenere questo risultato necessitava di un suo Virgilio come guida attraverso le liriche, e poi alla ricerca degli spazi reali; e questo Virgilio diventai io. Una volta a Roma, decidemmo di stabilire la nostra base di ricerca in un caffè di Trastevere; passando le mattinate a leggere e analizzare le poesie sicché Adam potesse afferrarne i dettagli tematici, e il ritmo

e la musicalità dei versi; dopo quest'operazione entrava in azione la macchina fotografica. Incessantemente, giorno e notte cercavamo di cogliere l'attimo giusto, la luce e le ombre che occupavano i cieli di Roma. Inutile dirlo, ma per me il tutto si rivelò essere un'esperienza di assoluta trasformazione, in quanto ho avuto modo di osservare in prima persona il lavoro della mente e dell'occhio di un bravo fotografo. Questo aspetto peculiare dell'elemento fotografico mi ha di sicuro offerto ulteriori strumenti per migliorare il mio lavoro di traduttore in italiano di Roma, pericolo per i viandanti.

Giuseppe Leporace

Non avrei mai previsto che questo mio primo incontro con Rafael Alberti a Roma si sarebbe rivelato essere l'inizio di una lunga e profonda amicizia. Nell'aprile del 1981 lo invitai a un simposio organizzato al Dartmouth College sull'arte e la letteratura della Guerra Civile Spagnola. In quell'occasione, Alberti mi affibbiò il soprannome di "Re dei Merovingi". L'anno seguente fu mio ospite a Granada dove trascorse una settimana memorabile nella mia abitazione. Un considerevole numero di suoi disegni ancora oggi adornano le pareti del mio ufficio e della mia casa a Seattle. In quell'occasione recitò all'interno del cortile del Palazzo de Puentezuelas, davanti a un gremito pubblico, le sue poesie "La ballata di colui che non andò mai a Granada", dedicate a Federico Garcia Lorca. Dopo la recita, gli organizzatori ci invitarono a visitare il burrone a Víznar dove Lorca fu assassinato da una squadra di fascisti.

Fra gli anni '80 e '90, quando mi capitava di andare a Madrid o a El Puerto de Santa Maria ci si rivedeva sempre. L'ultimo nostro incontro avvenne un anno o due prima della sua morte.

Anthony L. Geist

El lenguaje de la luz
Adam L.Weintraub

Smart cars. Teléfonos móviles. Zapatillas deportivas. Relojes digitales. Trolebuses. Marcas comerciales. Logos.

Como si fueran vecinos íntimos en el mercadillo del Campo dei Fiori, compitiendo por atraer tu ojo y atención—"Prueba el limoncello de fresas con jarabe de manzana y menta, ¡gratis, sin compromiso!"—estamos acostumbrados a las distracciones cotidianas actuales; es decir, lo escuchamos pero apenas prestamos atención. En realidad, eso sería cierto en cualquier época. En los tiempos que corren, saturados de imágenes y marcas comerciales, no nos damos cuenta de los obstáculos que pugnan hora tras hora por nuestra atención. Sobre todo en Roma.

Con mi colega y amigo, Giuseppe Leporace (co-fundador del concepto de esta edición), nos sentamos en la terraza del Caffè Belli en la Piazza Belli en el Trastévere, y leímos una y otra vez los poemas de Alberti intentando captar no solo la intención sino una inspiración de lo que pudiera representar fotográficamente cada poema. Como fotógrafo encargado de la interpretación de unos poemas del poeta gaditano extraordinariamente expresivos y particularmente visuales de Roma de los años 1960, al intentar crear un vínculo a través de cinco décadas de cambio en la "Città Eterna", la esencia y el fundamento de las palabras se me impusieron. Al intentar tender un puente a través del tiempo, la cultura contemporánea no solo me distraía en cada esquina, recoveco u obra maestra de Bellini, sino que lo invadía todo.

En mis visitas a la Ciudad Eterna me di cuenta cada vez más de que ese apodo era más bien engañoso. Desde la época de Alberti hasta hoy parece que ha pasado una eternidad y que sus palabras representan un tiempo más sencillo. Sin embargo, han quedado muchos detalles—y es allí donde he buscado un terreno en común: desde fotos en primer plano hasta momentos; en reliquias y relaciones.

Uno de mis primeros retos fue cómo hacer imágenes que esquivaran el paso del tiempo. Es decir, con todos los Smart cars atiborrados en cada calle, ¿cómo representar las motos en el Trastévere? Con todos los cachivaches destinados a turistas en el Campo dei Fiori, ¿cómo puedo captar la "imaginería" a la que se refiere Alberti? ¡Ya no existe!

Al cabo de un par de días me di cuenta de que solo había una manera de que esto funcionara: aceptar dónde estamos y quiénes somos—respetar los conceptos albertianos, no sus palabras exactas. Como han comprobado muchos traductores entre idiomas, estar atrapado en un intercambio palabra por palabra rara vez transmite verdadero significado. Me fue preciso reconocer que, de la misma manera en que muchas veces las referencias culturales se pierden en un intercambio literal, en el caso por ejemplo de un chiste, así también se perderían los conceptos de Alberti en esta traducción (usando el medio de la luz) si no nos adaptamos (¿aceptamos?) a las implicaciones contemporáneas de nuestra cultura.

De esa forma, en esta edición trilingüe del retrato que hace Alberti de su ciudad de adopción, procuro ser fiel a sus intenciones usando las herramientas (¡la luz!) que el momento me brindaba. Por favor, disculpen los cables que cuelgan. Disfruten el resplandor esporádico de un teléfono móvil. No hagan caso del Smart. Y regocíjense con la realidad de Roma, hoy, eternamente cambiante para futuras épocas. Y claro, todavía hay, en efecto, Vespas en el Trastévere.

Así tenemos un diálogo—más que una simple traducción de palabras en sentido literal—con otra época en las lenguas actuales. Las palabras de Alberti siguen reverberando con estoica emoción y sus intuiciones son sin duda eternas, si nos permitimos observar. Roma, sin embargo, evoluciona.

Il linguaggio della luce
Adam L. Weintraub

Smart cars. Cellulari. Scarpe da ginnastica. Orologi. Tram. Firme. Loghi aziendali.

Come se queste cose fossero intimi vicinati al mercato di Campo de' Fiori, in competizione per un tuo sguardo e attenzione—"assaggia questo limoncello alla fragola con sciroppo di mela e menta, gratis e senza obbligazioni!"—siamo assuefatti alle tentazioni quotidiane; cioè ascoltiamo senza veramente sentirle. In verità questo atteggiamento è valido da sempre. Nell'era odiena, saturata da immagini e incentrata sul marchio, ignoriamo le contraddizioni in contrapposizione per la nostra attenzione in ogni istante. Sopratutto se siamo a Roma.

Con il collega ed amico Giuseppe Leporace (co-ideatore del concetto di questa edizione), siamo seduti a un tavolino del Caffè Belli in Piazza Belli a Trastevere, a leggere e rileggere le liriche di Alberti cercando di coglierne e catturarne non solo l'intento, ma sopratutto un'ispirazione per ciò che potrebbe, dal punto di vista fotografico, rappresentare ogni singolo componimento. Dal momento che come fotografo ho l'onore e l'onere di offrire un'interpretazione delle meravigliosamente espressive poesie di Alberti nella Roma degli anni '60, allo scopo di creare un legame che trasporti i cambiamenti avvenuti nella "Città Eterna" attraverso decine e decine di anni trascorsi, la vera essenza e il fondamento delle parole è diventato fondamentalmente cruciale. In questo tentativo di collegare il tempo nel tempo, la cultura del vissuto quotidiano non solo distrae ad ogni angolo, nicchia o capolavoro di Bellini, ma molto frequentemente invade il campo.

Durante le mie varie permanenze nella Città Eterna, mi è apparso ovvio che questo nome non è altro che una definizione ingannevole. Dai tempi di Alberti ad oggi, sembra che sia passata un'eternità, e che le sue parole sono il simbolo di tempi più semplici. Nonostante le tante mutazioni avvenute, tantissimi dettagli ne sono ancora testimonio—ed è proprio lì dove ogni mio sforzo sarà di trovare un terreno comune: da primi piani a momenti; in reliche e relazioni.

Uno dei miei conflitti iniziali è stato: come creare immagini capaci di rappresentare lo spostamento del tempo? In poche parole, con tutte le Smart car ammassate in ogni strada, come posso far vedere le Vespe a Trastevere? Con tutta la pacchianeria per turisti in vendita sulle bancarelle di Campo de' Fiori, come posso far vedere le cianfrusaglie di un altro tempo? Non ci sono più!

Solo dopo alcuni giorni mi è venuto da pensare che c'era un solo modo per riuscire in questa impresa: accettare il tempo in cui ci troviamo e ciò che nel tempo siamo diventati-onorando i concetti di Alberti e non le sue precise parole.

Ogni buon traduttore è consapevole del fatto che restare intrappolati in uno scambio linguistico che avviene nel senso letterale, spesso sacrifica lo scopo inteso nell'opera in lingua originale. Anche io ho dovuto riconoscere questo dettaglio in quanto i riferimenti culturali spesso si perdono in uno scambio parola-per-parola, come ad esempio avviene nella comprensione di una barzelletta, e cosi avverrebbe ai concetti di Alberti, i quali sarebbero sacrificati in una simile traduzione (usando il medium della luce), se non ci si sforza di (accettarele implicazioni culturali della contemporanetà.

Quindi, in questa edizione trilingua del ritratto che Alberti offre della sua città adottiva, il mio sforzo costante è quello di rimanere fedele allo scopo dell'autore, facendo uso di qualsiasi strumento (luce!) offertomi dal momento. Chiedo venia per i tanti fili lasciati in sospeso! Godiamoci il bagliore occasionale di uno smart phone! Ignoriamo le Smart car! E dilettiamoci nella realtà di Roma, oggi, eternamente in mutazione per le epoche a venire. Ovviamente, ancora si vedono, infatti, le Vespa a Trastevere.

Dunque, qui intercorre un dialogo—e non una traduzione di parole in senso letterale—di un altro tempo, ma nel linguaggio dei giorni nostri. Le parole di Alberti continuano a riverberare con stoica intensa emozione, e le sue intuizioni sono sicuramente eterne, se noi desideriamo appropriarcene. Roma, comunque, è in continuo divenire.

Autores
Authors
Autori

Poeta

Poeta

Rafael Alberti nace y muere con el siglo xx. Ve la luz en el Puerto de Santa María en 1902 y allí fallece en 1999, cerrando el círculo. Miembro de la mítica generación del 27, fue un poeta prolífico, autor más de 30 libros de poesía. Su poesía nace bajo el signo de la nostalgia, nostalgia de aquello que ha tenido que dejar atrás en sus sucesivos exilios: de la luminosa bahía de Cádiz a Madrid a los 15 años; de Madrid a París al final de la Guerra Civil en 1939, con su mujer María Teresa León y, un año más tarde, de allí a Argentina. En 1963 se ve obligado a abandonar el país por un gobierno peronista de derechas y se establece en Roma, donde permanece hasta que, por fin, puede volver a España en 1977. Con todo, sigue creando—poesía, teatro, memorias, dibujos, poemas caligrafiados—que perduran y perdurarán, formando parte del acervo cultural para hoy y mañana.

Rafael Alberti nasce e muore nel ventesimo secolo. Aprì gli occhi per la prima volta a El Puerto de Santa Maria, e chiuse il cerchio della sua vita ancora lì, spegnendosi per sempre nel 1999. Ebbe parte attiva nella mitica Generazione del '27, fu poeta prolifico: dalla sua penna uscirono più di 30 raccolte di poesie. La sua poesia nasce sotto il segno della nostalgia; nostalgia per tutto ciò che era stato costretto a lasciarsi dietro a causa del forzato esilio: dalla luminosa cittadina di Cadige a Madrid durante la sua adolescenza; da Madrid a Parigi con sua moglie Maria Teresa Leon, alla fine della Guerra Civile Spagnola del 1939, e, un anno dopo, da lì salpare per l'Argentina. Nel 1963 fu scacciato anche da quel paese dal suo governo di destra e si stabilì a Roma, dove visse fino a quando gli fu permesso il rientro in terra di Spagna nel 1977. In tutto questo caos esistenziale continuò a coltivare il suo spirito creativo—poesia, teatro, memoirs, disegni, poesie scritte a mano—che continueranno a testimoniare ora e per sempre il suo spirito creativo all'interno della nostra tradizione culturale presente e futura.

Traductores

Esta edición de *Roma, peligro para caminantes* es el fruto de un sueño compartido. Se basa en una selección de poemas de la primera edición (México: Joaquín Mortiz, 1968). Presenta la primera traducción al inglés de este icónico poemario, junto con una nueva y novedosa versión italiana de los versos romanos de Alberti, en diálogo con una serie de sorprendentes y emotivas fotos de la Città Eterna.

Anthony L. Geist, autor de las versiones en inglés, es profesor de Literatura Española en la Universidad de Washington (Seattle). Sus traducciones del poeta peruano Luis Hernández quedaron finalistas en el Premio PEN (2016). Se siente afortunado que dos de sus grandes pasiones—el estudio de la poesía y la guerra civil española—también sean su profesión.

Giuseppe Leporace, profesor adjunto de Estudios Italianos en la Universidad de Washington, jubilado en 2018, ahora está felizmente de vuelta en Italia, al norte de Roma, donde vive con su mujer y sus dos hijos. Comparte el gusto por la enseñanza con el placer de la traducción literaria. Ha traducido al inglés la obra completa de la poeta italiana Amelia Rosselli y una selección de poemas de Mark Strand al italiano.

Adam L. Weintraub, originario de Seattle, habiendo vivido dos años y medio en Italia y 20 años casado con una peruana, es lógico que colabore en un libro trilingüe. Es un fotógrafo profesional que también organiza tours fotográficos y culinarios. Y da vueltas por el centro de Roma con una cámara. Y una copa de vino.

Traduttori

Questa edizione di *Roma, pericolo per i viandanti* è frutto di un sogno condiviso. Si basa su una selezione di poesie della prima edizione (Messico: Joaquín Mortiz, 1968). Offre la prima traduzione in inglese di questa iconografica raccolta di poesie e una nuova e originale versione italiana dei versi romani di Alberti, in dialogo con sorprendenti e commoventi immagini fotografiche della Città Eterna.

Anthony L. Geist, autore della versione in inglese, è professore ordinario di letteratura spagnola presso l'Università di Washington. La sua traduzione del poeta peruviano Luis Hernández fu finalista del PEN Prize nel 2016. Si considera baciato dalla fortuna perchè le due sue grandi passioni—poesia e la Guerra Civile Spagnola—sono parte complementare della sua professione.

Giuseppe Leporace, professore aggiunto presso il dipartimento di Italianistica dell'Università di Washington a Seattle, in pensione dal 2018, e ora felicemente ritornato in Italia con moglie e i due figli, a nord di Roma. Oltre all'amore per l'insegnamento, ha sempre coltivato un profondo interesse per la traduzione letteraria. Fra i suoi lavori di traduzione si è occupato dell'opera di Amelia Rosselli in inglese, e ha pubblicato in italiano una selezione delle poesie di Mark Strand.

Adam L. Weintraub, originario di Seattle, passa due anni e mezzo in Italia, e gli ultimi venti felicemente sposato con una meravigliosa peruviana, è congeniale per un'edizione trilingue di questa dimensione. La sua occupazione principale e quella di fotografo professionista e di produttore di tour di viaggi avventurosi. E anche quella di girare incessantemente per il centro di Roma in compagnia della sua macchina fotografica, e di un buon bicchiere di vino.

When I leave Rome...

Swan Isle Press is a not-for-profit publisher of literature
in translation including fiction, nonfiction, and poetry.

For information on books of related interest
or for a catalog of Swan Isle Press titles:
www.swanislepress.com